Aspects of Early New York Society and Politics

ASPECTS
OF EARLY NEW YORK
SOCIETY AND POLITICS

*Edited by Jacob Judd
and Irwin H. Polishook*

SLEEPY HOLLOW RESTORATIONS

TARRYTOWN · NEW YORK

Library of Congress Cataloging in Publication Data
Main entry under title:
Aspects of early New York society and politics.
Papers presented at a conference held in
Tarrytown, N. Y., Oct. 1-2, 1971, and
sponsored by Sleepy Hollow Restorations.
Bibliography: p.
1. New York (State)—Politics and government—Colonial period—Congresses.
2. New York (State)—History—Colonial period—Congresses.
I. Judd, Jacob, 1929–   ed.
II. Polishook, Irwin H., ed.
III. Sleepy Hollow Restorations, Tarrytown, N. Y.
F122.A84   974.7'02   73-6579
ISBN 0-912882-06-9

F
122
.A84

ISBN 0-912882-06-9
Library of Congress Catalog Card Number: 73-6579
First Printing
Printed in the United States of America

CONTENTS

ILLUSTRATIONS   *vi*

PREFACE   *vii*

New York: Municipality and Province   1
    Jacob Judd

New York in the American Colonies: A New Look   8
    Milton M. Klein

Local Government in Colonial New York:
A Base for Republicanism   29
    Patricia U. Bonomi

New York: Prototype of Modern America   51
    Lawrence H. Leder

Quantification and New York History   57
    Irwin H. Polishook

The Age of Leisler—New York City, 1689–1710:
A Social and Demographic Interpretation   63
    Thomas J. Archdeacon

Military Experience and the Origins of Federalism
and Antifederalism   83
    Edwin G. Burrows

Commentary by *Jackson Turner Main*   93

The American Revolution Comes to John Jay   96
    Richard B. Morris

APPENDIX   118

NOTES   132

FURTHER READINGS   144

CONTRIBUTORS   145

INDEX   147

1290567

ILLUSTRATIONS

A Plan of the City of New York, circa 1730   3

Portrait of Richard Coote, Earl of Bellomont   9

First meeting place of New York Senate in
Kingston, New York   31

Portrait of Edward Hyde, Lord Cornbury   53

A Plan of the Harbour of New York, circa 1730   59

A View of the New Dutch Church in New York City,
circa 1731   65

Newspaper announcement of the raising of a battalion
of Continental soldiers in New York, July 27, 1775   85

The "Labadist" view of New York, circa 1679–1680   94

Portrait of John Jay by John Trumbull   97

PREFACE

As PART of its educational service to the academic community and the general public, Sleepy Hollow Restorations sponsors occasional conferences in various aspects of American history, and one such conference was held on October 1 and 2, 1971 in Tarrytown, New York. Some two hundred scholars attended the meetings.

The overall subject for the conference was New York history, emphasizing the colonial and Revolutionary eras. Two formal sessions were arranged, "Society in Early New York," and "The New York Political Scene," with papers by Thomas J. Archdeacon of the University of Wisconsin at Madison; Edwin G. Burrows, now of Brooklyn College of the City University of New York; Milton M. Klein, University of Tennessee; and Patricia U. Bonomi of New York University. At a dinner meeting on October 1, Richard B. Morris, Gouverneur Morris Professor of History at Columbia University, presented an address on "The American Revolution Comes to John Jay." Commentators for the two formal sessions were Jackson Turner Main, State University of New York at Stony Brook; and Lawrence H. Leder, Lehigh University. Brooke Hindle of New York University and the two editors served as a program committee for the organization of the conference.

All the papers presented at the conference are published here in much the same form though not the same order in which they were first delivered. In each instance, other than Morris' study which is based primarily on the Jay Papers, the full documentation inappropriate to an oral presentation has been added. The program committee's initial conception was to secure papers for this conference that would give some evidence of the quality of ongoing research in New York history as well as make a contribution in their own terms. No attempt was made to organize the proceedings around a single theme. We hope that the published volume realizes in some measure our original intentions.

JACOB JUDD

IRWIN H. POLISHOOK

Herbert H. Lehman College
of the City University of New York

New York: Municipality and Province

Jacob Judd

I f the Duke of York and his "servant" Richard Nicolls had originally designated the town at the southern end of the province as Manhattan, or by some other Indian correlative, much historical confusion might have been avoided. Frequently scholars have tended to misconstrue the municipality with the province of New York. This has led to indiscriminate assumptions concerning economic propensities, demographic modifications, political relationships, and cultural life-styles within the two areas. Had there been a difference in nomenclature, it might have been easier to differentiate trends associated with urbanization in a given area as contrasted with those forces related to an agricultural and extractive economy.

Though scholars have, on occasion, lost sight of the distinctiveness between the two regions, the inhabitants did not. Early in the Dutch period settlers in the two major enclaves of Fort Amsterdam and Fort Orange sought extraordinary trading privileges for themselves on the basis of their economic uniqueness. Their request was acceded to when The West India Company created the Great and Small burgher rights in 1657. These special trading advantages were granted because the Company recognized that the inhabitants of New Amsterdam thought in terms of a commercial opportunism and expansion which would redound eventually to the benefit of the Company's coffers.

Almost from the outset New Amsterdam's inhabitants were dissatisfied with the meager trading opportunities presented to them in furs, grain, and fish within a Company-controlled situation. As soon as they were granted the chance, settlers of New Amsterdam became merchants involved in acquiring tobacco

1

and dye woods as part of a coastal trade while expanding market opportunities for New Netherland's products.

English occupation enhanced the activities of the city merchants. They benefited from being included in England's sphere as well as continuing, in a modified form, the traditional trade with the Netherlands. It soon resulted in the city merchants developing an international commerce, with New York-registered vessels appearing in the major trade areas of the world. Even before the end of the seventeenth century there emerged New York shipping magnates who controlled far-flung mercantile empires.

Perhaps the most outstanding figures were the Philipses, father and son, Frederick and Adolph. Beginning life in New Amsterdam as the West India Company's carpenter, Frederick (born Vrydrich Flypsen) sought every opportunity to advance a career in commerce. Marrying an extremely wealthy widow who possessed a well-organized fleet of merchant vessels, Frederick soon built it up to a formidable one. By the 1690's his ships called at islands in the West Indies, the Madeiras, Oporto, the ports of England and Holland, at Hamburg, both coasts of Africa, the islands of the Indian Ocean, and, closer to home, all along the North American Atlantic seacoast.

Frederick Philipse's civic services ranged from being a local arbitrator to serving on the governors' council. His civic and political activities gradually progressed from the municipal to the provincial level in keeping with his expanded wealth, prestige, and need for contacts. As far as the Philipses were concerned, their mercantile activities were of such magnitude that only at the provincial level could they acquire and achieve the necessary support for their myriad trade interests.

This in itself points up a very important characteristic of the political development of the city. The city was the political child of the province in that the city achieved separate governmental status as the result of a governor's decree. The corporate composition, the general principles under which it operated, and the budget of the municipality were controlled, to a great extent, by the province. It was the province which established rules and

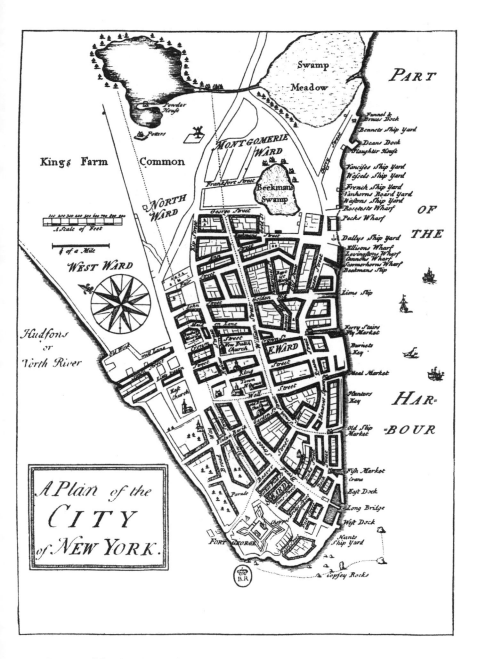

Engraved by I. Carwithan, ca. 1730. Original in
the Bibliotheque Nationale, Paris.

regulations concerning commerce and trade, the use of dock and wharf facilities, the payments of imposts, and general trade conduct. The city and the province, though separate in economic outlook and style of life, still existed together in a reciprocal situation born of a common political structure. Therefore, it was incumbent upon the Philipses to seek influence on the provincial level rather than in the municipality.

Not every inhabitant of the city, however, was a Philipse. The average denizen who engaged in a craft or provided brawn was not concerned with the issues of import regulations and wharfage fees. His interests were more fundamental and in keeping with the basic concepts behind the establishment of government, that is, the protection of life and property. He wanted the municipality to provide him with adequate police and fire protection, some form of sanitation service, a water supply, and a guarantee of his property rights.

As early as Peter Stuyvesant's day, it was recognized that no matter how loath municipal fathers might be to enter into such activities, the well-being of the community would force them into some action. Stumbling, making many false starts and errors, the city of New York began to evolve methods of dealing with these problems. They had not been resolved by the time of the Revolution (and, of course, they are still with us today in far more complex forms), yet efforts to cope with the unique problems associated with urban living had begun.

An interesting problem of research and analysis concerning urban development in New York would involve a study of the efforts of later urban settlements within the state to deal with municipal services. Did they benefit from the earlier experiences of New York City? Did they attempt to recreate on a smaller scale the city's efforts at problem-solving? Or, did they ignore Gotham's achievements and strike out on their own? How were urban centers in adjacent colonies influenced by New York City? A large body of documentation exists for such a study and could lead to some important conclusions. More generally, in urban development, have we learned from past mistakes and accomplishments?

The history of New York was not only commercial but agricultural as well. New York is currently the second most important dairy state in the nation. During the colonial period its main thrust was agricultural combined with the extractive products of the land and forests: furs, timber, naval stores, iron, and lime. Quite often agricultural and commercial pursuits were united in one individual or family. Here again, the Philipses are an excellent example. After having acquired wealth from commercial ventures, the family began to purchase tracts of land in the province. By the end of the 1600's they had acquired over 90,000 acres of prime Westchester County property stretching along the east bank of the Hudson River from Spuyten Duyvil to the Croton River. They wasted no time in establishing grist and saw mills within their extensive holdings. The reconstructed Tarrytown mill is a significant reminder of this diversification. Their own properties provided them with furs, lumber, lime, and quantities of grain for exportation. Primarily interested at first in trade and commerce, they soon learned to regard agricultural activities as part of their business enterprises. They controlled the raising, packing and preparing, shipping, and final sale of products emanating from their domain. Should they be regarded as manorial lords whose main thrust was toward the soil, or as early business entrepreneurs who had created a colonial conglomerate?

It is in this wider context of commercial outlook, development of agriculture as a business, provincial politics, and urbanization, all acting simultaneously in union and as disparate forces, which makes New York's history unique. Milton M. Klein in his essay, "New York in the American Colonies: A New Look," stresses the absence of an adequate synthesis of New York's colonial role. He points out that a goodly number of studies concerned with colonial development either ignore New York's uniqueness or attempt to hide the province within a general and misleading Middle Atlantic grouping. This has been a result of a lack of understanding regarding New York's atypicality or has arisen from a rudimentary awareness that the province does not fit into preconceived notions regarding the North American colonies.

Klein contends that New York should receive its rightful place in American historiography as being "prototypical," in that its population was so heterogeneous, religious differences were tolerated, and its economy varied. It also had a strategic importance second to none, and a political scene most confusing not only to those who lived through the period but to later-day historians as well.

Patricia U. Bonomi's essay, "Local Government in Colonial New York: A Base for Republicanism," also stresses the failure of scholars to emphasize and develop properly the complicated history of the middle colonies. Furthermore, Bonomi points out that an area of investigation profoundly neglected for the New York colony has been local institutional history. Her suggestions that this shortcoming stems from the problem of dealing with the diversity and multiplicity of governmental bodies in New York and from the difficulty in obtaining adequate research materials are valid. They confirm Klein's complaints about the inadequacy of the prevailing historiography. Lawrence H. Leder also echoes this view, asserting that the county and town archives of New York were in a deplorable condition as recently as a decade ago. It is only within recent years that efforts have been introduced to salvage and organize the colonial records scattered throughout the State.

The town government of Kingston is the main focus of Bonomi's study. What kind of political structure evolved at the local level; who assumed the governmental leadership; and, to what extent did local citizens participate in government? These are the problems she has successfully analyzed and resolved for us. Her conclusion that local inhabitants from all walks of life were chosen to participate in local government squares with the conclusions of other scholars who have studied local participation in the nineteenth century.

From whom could the local inhabitants choose? As Bonomi indicates, the equivalent of the English country squire did not develop in New York province; hence, customs for selecting political leaders evolved in the new world colony. In assessing the worth of one's neighbors, it became important to think beyond

material values and possessions and to examine their intelligence, diligence, and trustworthiness. It mattered not whether
the man was a cobbler or a lawyer. What proved important were
intrinsic values of work habits, willingness to participate, and re-
liability. Those who possessed these traits found opportunities to
rise rapidly in local politics.

The opportunity to participate in government at the local level
by inhabitants who, in the mother countries would not have
been deemed worthy of such a state, was revolutionary in itself.
It was this that helped make the American colonies unique. The
local butcher and baker were directly involved in decision-making and in the process learned to rely on themselves.

This close-knit relationship also led to a parochialism which,
Bonomi declares, should be regarded in a positive sense. As she
so aptly states, "it may well have been this very parochialism, its
very narrowness of view, its suspiciousness, its jealous attachment to local prerogatives, that furnished the vital ingredient
and much of the staying power to the Americans' revolutionary
and, later, to their republican consciousness."

The problems facing the inhabitants of Kingston Township
were of a nature inherent in the development of urbanization.
Their problems and the solutions reached were similar to New
York City's situation at an earlier time. It is unfortunate that the
debates of the trustees' meetings do not exist, for they might
have cast light on whether the Kingstonites knew of New York
City's earlier struggles and efforts to resolve problems of a very
similar nature. What made Kingston unique was that it was primarily agricultural while, at the same time, it was developing as
a commercial center on the Hudson River.

New York in the American Colonies: A New Look

Milton M. Klein

I

On every occasion of the anniversary of the founding of Jamestown or the landing at Plymouth, heated debate occurs— more often among amateur than among professional historians —as to which of these two events more properly marks the beginning of the American epic. On the 350th commemoration of the arrival of the *Susan Constant* and her sister ships, a southern partisan, Virginius Dabney, was especially vocal in raising the query: "Why have historians underrated the Virginia Fathers?" Justice for the southern colonies, he cried! New Englanders ignored the plea and arranged to have a reconstruction of the *Mayflower* brought to Plymouth on *its* 350th birthday. The war promises to be one of those unending historical conflicts. What I propose to do is not settle the question but confuse it further— by simply suggesting that we correct the myopia of both sides, reject the claims of each, and offer a new contender for the honor of initiating the American tradition; the Middle Colonies, in general, and New York more particularly.

The early neglect of Americans in turning elsewhere than New York for their national image is not hard to understand. The American colonies were founded once by the first settlers, and as Wesley Craven has observed, the process was repeated over and over again as succeeding generations redrew the portrait of the Founding Fathers to suit their own moods. But whatever the angle of vision of these varying recreations of the nature of our

8

Richard Coote, Earl of Bellomont, Governor of New York, 1697–1701. Portrait owned by Mr. & Mrs. Jack M. Coote, London, England. *Photograph courtesy of The New-York Historical Society, New York City.*

colonial origins, New York was ignored. A perceptive explanation of this neglect has been offered by two sociologists in a recent book on New York City:[1]

> History, or perhaps historians, keep passing New York by. . . . By preference, but also in some degree by necessity, America has turned elsewhere for its images and traditions. Colonial America is preserved for us in terms of the Doric simplicity of New England, or the pastoral symmetry of the Virginia countryside. . . . But who can summon an image of eighteenth-century New York that will still hold in the mind?

There are other explanations, historical and historiographical. The earliest American historians reflected the regional consciousness of New England and Virginia. Historical accounts of these geographic areas appeared within 75 years of their founding, even if "New England" was more often synonymous with Massachusetts and "Virginia" broadly construed. The histories of the southern colonies stressed the great achievement of the Virginia charters in bringing English liberties and common law to these shores at so early a date. New Englanders emphasized the divine Providence which had guided Pilgrims and Puritans and thereby set the providential tone for all future American development.[2] New York's beginnings as a conquered province and the proprietary of the King's brother could stir few patriotic breasts and arouse little native emotion. As the Revolution approached, the polemicists of Boston and Williamsburg found solid precedent for their claims to English liberties in their first charters and in the images they created of their first settlers, whom they represented as early exponents of liberty and opponents of tyranny. New York had no such charter to cite as comparable example.

After independence, the earliest national histories linked Virginians and New Englanders as common progenitors of "the just and genuine principles" of the new republican society. Portraying our national origins as rooted in the rising of a free people, "not led by powerful families," and "under no general influence, but that of their personal feelings and opinions," who had already achieved a republican society before the separation from England, these historians steered clear of New York, with its aristocratic manor lords, great estates, and quasi-feudal tenantry as illustrations of the indigenous republican spirit.³ That New York was one of the least militant and most hesitant of the provinces in casting its vote for independence did not improve its standing with future historians from New England. William Gordon's *History*, published in 1789, specifically disavowed the role of New York, with its "party of aristocracy," in the glorious struggle against tyranny.⁴

Local historians of New York did little to help its reputation. Washington Irving's *New York* was a caricature which infuriated the state's better citizenry. Thomas Jones's loyalist *History of New York*, appearing in 1879, proved no better, since it represented the province's "golden age" as those halcyon days of the mid-eighteenth century just before the evil triumvirate of Presbyterians and lawyers—William Livingston, William Smith, Jr., and John Morin Scott—began their conspiracy to turn the colony on its head by its agitation against church and state. When biography replaced history as the favorite literary medium for recalling the nation's heritage, again New York suffered. It had no heroes of the stature of Washington and Patrick Henry to eulogize.

In creating a "usable past" for a new people, the homogeneous English communities of New England and the South had far more appeal than New York's (or New Jersey's or Pennsylvania's) disordered, complex, heterogeneous population. Indeed, the more ethnically varied America became in the years that followed, the more attractive did Anglo-Saxon Jamestown and Plymouth appear to historians who themselves were disturbed by, and hostile to, the influx of masses of European immigrants from outside the British Isles or its northern neighbors. Thus, John Fiske, a convert to the theory of the Teutonic origins of American democracy and of Aryan race supremacy, traced the roots of our political heritage from the primitive Saxons through the English middle class and then to America in the veins of Virginia Cavaliers and New England Puritans. A limited degree of heterogeneity was acceptable, since the English race had a "rare capacity for absorbing slightly foreign elements and molding them into conformity" with Anglo-Saxon political ideals. Hence, Fiske was prevented from rejecting the Dutch, Huguenots, Jews, Germans, and Scotch-Irish who comprised so much of the population of the Middle Colonies. It is quite clear, however, from Fiske's strong hostility to late nineteenth-century immigration—he was President of the Immigration Restriction League—that New York's mongrel people took only second place in his roll of proper Americans.[5]

Even when the study of immigration was made professionally respectable by Marcus Lee Hansen, the focus was on the immigrants who peopled the rural Midwest, not those who crowded New York's urban ghettos.[6] Popular rhetoric glorified the country as a melting pot of different peoples, but in actuality what was meant was the degree to which immigrants conformed to Anglo-Saxon characteristics.

Geography, also, had something to do with the neglect of the Middle Colonies. They could not be clearly defined, nor were the Middle Atlantic States much easier afterwards. At times, British administrators simply swallowed up the middle region into the other two, using the term "northern colonies" to include New England, New York, New Jersey, and Pennsylvania. Cartographers confused the matter similarly. Lewis Evans, in his famous map of 1755, depicted the Middle Colonies as including everything from Virginia to Rhode Island! With the Middle Atlantic region undefinable physically, it is not surprising that historians failed to write about it. Except for Fiske's two volumes on the Dutch and Quaker colonies, published in 1899, nothing appeared on the subject until Wertenbaker's volume in his *Founding of American Civilization* series in 1938; and no study of the Middle Atlantic States found its way into print until 1956.[7]

Richard Shryock has raised the provocative question of whether historians have neglected the Middle Atlantic region—either as colonies or as states—because it does not exist or whether the region has been lost to view because historians have failed to write about it.[8] One interesting suggestion he offers for the blurred focus of historians is that the inhabitants of the area have never developed the kind of regional self-consciousness

which arises from the nursing of a grievance. Certainly there is
nothing in Middle Atlantic history comparable to C. Vann
Woodward's "Burden of Southern History"—the brooding sense
of racial guilt and consciousness of military defeat. Nor is there
evidence of anything like the anguished cry of an alienated social elite—such as David Donald's New England Abolitionists.
In recalling its origins, the Middle Colonies could not draw upon
the knowledge of a "starving time" which its first settlers had
overcome by stubborn will or divine intervention. Nor could the
Middle Colonies attribute the formation of their collective character to the forge of bitter encounters with savages during their
earliest years. There were no counterparts to the New Englanders' fierce conflicts with the Pequots and Narragansetts, in 1637
and 1675–76, nor to Virginia's Indian massacres of 1622 and
1644 in the recollection of New Yorkers and Pennsylvanians.
Conflict with the Indians was not entirely absent in the history
of these colonies, but the diplomatic skill of a Penn and the business acumen of the Dutch had secured a peace through trade
and diplomacy which kept the Middle Colonies free from the
worst horrors of Indian warfare—and made them the object of
suspicion and envy. Economically, New York and its neighbors,
by the eve of the Revolution, enjoyed so large a measure of prosperity that one historian offers this condition, along with the colonies' social and cultural diversity, as an explanation of their in-
decision for independence, in contrast to New England and Virginia, whose impaired economic fortunes propelled them the
more rapidly toward a separation which their socially homogeneous populations could be asked to accept.[9]

Clearly, however, it was the urban character of the Middle
Colonies, symbolized by the great cities of New York and Philadelphia, and their polyglot populations which played a major
role in the historical amnesia of Americans, who preferred to remember their homogeneous, rural Arcadia even as it disappeared
before their eyes. The paradox, of course, was that colonies like
New York represented, in germinal form, the very nation that
had come into existence by the late nineteenth century. The paradox is heightened by the discovery that the historian who, more

than any other, was responsible for focusing the nation's attention on its rural West as the home of its distinctive traits of collective character should also have been the one to stress most emphatically the Middle Atlantic origins of those traits.

A year before his famous essay on the significance of the frontier, Frederick Jackson Turner directed the notice of historians to the "middle region" of the Atlantic coast and deplored the fact that it had "never been studied with the care due to its importance." With its wide mixture of nationalities, he noted, its varied society and economic life, its multiplicity of religions, and its mixed pattern of town and county government, the region between New England and the South represented for Turner "that composite" which was the America of 1892, even the patterns of its settlement reflecting the map of Europe in variety. The region was also "typical of the modern United States" in its ideas and ideals: democratic, national, easy, tolerant, and strongly materialistic.[10] In the frontier address itself, Turner repeated his sentiments in more explicit fashion. It was the very non-Englishness of the middle region which made it "typically American." It "mediated" between East and West, between Puritan New England and the slaveholding South; and it was the least sectional of all the sections. The men of the frontier, whom Turner eulogized, "had closer resemblances to the Middle region than to either of the other sections."[11]

The more Turner wrote about the West and on sectionalism, the more he seemed to return to the importance of the Middle Atlantic area. In two subsequent essays, he reiterated the prototypicality of the Middle Colonies and States for their composite nationality and democratic social structure:

> The middle region was so complex in its composition that it had little social self-consciousness as a section. Nevertheless this region of many nationalities, creeds, and industries became, during a considerable part of its history, a more characteristically democratic region than any of the others. Tolerance of difference of opinion was pronounced, and, in the course of time, individualism and lack of social control became marked features of the section.[12]

In a florid metaphor, Turner painted the West as a land of new "national hue," a composite coloration of all of its eastern ingredients and its local environment, but one section gave the distinctive tint to the new color: "This section was the Middle Region." In the posthumous volume, *The United States, 1830–1850,* Turner again stressed the special "national destiny" of the Middle Atlantic, its leadership by 1830 in urban growth, manufacturing, and shipping, its perfect reflection of the American "melting pot," and its pivotal role in the nation's politics—all of which made it for him "typical of the deep-seated tendencies of America in general."[13]

One of Turner's colleagues, Woodrow Wilson, agreed that the region between New England and the South was more than merely a blurred middle ground between two more important extremes. In outlining the course of American development, Wilson challenged the notion that the country's history comprised the working out of Puritan and southern ideals, each striving for predominance. It was, in fact, New York, New Jersey, and Pennsylvania which by their composite character and origins presaged later complex America. Here, according to Wilson, occurred the experiments that most resembled the methods by which the American continent was peopled; in the Middle Atlantic States, from the beginning, life reflected the pattern of living of the nation itself.[14]

Turner and Wilson were exceptional, and none of Turner's students except Carl Becker were attracted either to the Middle Colonies or the Middle States as fields of research. Becker himself found trouble blending the frontier thesis of his mentor into his own interpretation of the urban origins of colonial democracy. For other American historians, the very resemblance of the Middle Atlantic region to the nation as a whole produced a familiarity that bred only indifference, not scholarly attraction. Still others were baffled by the very qualities of life and culture in the Middle Colonies that did not set them apart from the rest of the nation. A region that appeared to be "everyman's" became "no man's" in literature and history.[15]

Present-day historians undertaking to achieve a synthesis of the colonial period have yet to spell out New York's role satisfactorily. In the most recent such effort, Daniel Boorstin illustrates his underlying theme of practical adaptation by reference to the experiences of Massachusetts, Virginia, Pennsylvania, and Georgia. New York, despite its overridingly accommodative political and religious structure and its pragmatic society and culture, is unmentioned. The elements in synthesizing New York (and the Middle Colonies) into the stream of early American history are perfectly visible; and it is the purpose of this essay to point out some directions which such inquiry should logically take.

II

The central fact in the colony's history, so well observed even by historians who have slighted it, is the heterogeneity of its population. This circumstance arose from the nature of the colony's beginning as an English province, the absorption of some 10,000 residents of New Netherland. But the population had already developed a diversity under Dutch rule which adumbrated its later heterogeneity. There were in New Netherland—besides Hollanders—Walloons, Swedes, English, Norwegians, Germans, Scotch-Irish, and Negroes. The visiting Jesuit, Father Jogues, was astonished to be told in 1644 that 18 languages were spoken in the province. This diversity was a cause for continued amazement on the part of English officials and visitors, the substitution of English for Dutch rule doing nothing to improve the homogeneity of the colony's population. One traveler in 1760 abandoned any attempt to generalize about New Yorkers: "Being . . . of different nations, different languages and different religions, it is almost impossible to give them any precise or determinate character."[16] On the eve of the Revolution, the population of the colony was estimated to be still only half English, making New York the most polygenetic of all the British dependencies in North America. The consequence of this diversity was enormous for the religious, political, and cultural life of the province, as it was for the later United States.

It is now clear that while this country can take credit for its faith in freedom of religion, the prize did not come as a free gift or as an act of love from our earliest forebears. The English came with established ideas of religious orthodoxy and conformity in their intellectual and spiritual baggage, nor was this heritage changed much by the New England Protestantism which Burke hailed as "the dissidence of dissent." Religious liberty was rather extorted step-by-step from an unwilling majority and accorded ultimately less out of commitment than as a result of social and economic necessity. Nowhere did the process evolve more typically than in New York. With its social complexity came religious diversity almost from the beginning. The domines of the Dutch Reformed Church were no more liberal in matters of religion than the spiritual representatives of the English conquerors. Toleration became the New Netherland way because of the pragmatic outlook of the Dutch West India Company. When crusty Peter Stuyvesant recommended, shortly after the arrival of the first Jews, that these "blasphemers of Christ" be barred from the colony, he was advised to allow them and the Lutherans, whom the Director-General found almost as objectionable, to "peacefully carry on their business" and to treat both sects "quietly and leniently." That Jews in Amsterdam reminded the company of the loyal support extended by their coreligionists in defense of the Dutch settlement in Brazil was helpful, but what was even more persuasive was the capital which Dutch Jews had invested in the company and the knowledge that the American plantation was underpopulated. "The more of loyal people that go to live there, the better it is in regard to the population of the country . . . and in regard to the increase of trade," the Amsterdam Chamber was reminded. So the Jews were permitted to stay and by struggle wrested from the government the right to a burial ground, exemption from Sabbath business laws, and service in the militia.[17]

When Stuyvesant, undaunted, turned his intolerance against Quakers, he prompted not only a stiffer rebuke from home but also evoked one of the most moving expressions of the principle of religious freedom in our history. With Quakers swarming over Long Island, the governor thought to hound them away by prohibiting the other inhabitants from admitting them into their

homes, whereupon 31 shocked residents of Flushing subscribed
to the following remonstrance:[18]

Right Honorable
   You have been pleased to send up unto us a certain prohibition or
command that we should not receive or entertain any of those people
called Quakers because they are supposed to be by some seducers of
the people. For our part we cannot condemn them in this case neither
can we stretch out our hands against them to punish, banish, or perse-
cute them, for out of Christ God is a consuming fire, and it is a fearful
[thing] to fall into the hands of the living God.
   We desire therefore in this case not to judge least we be judged,
neither to condemn least we be condemned, but rather [to] let every
man stand and fall to his own Master. We are bound by the law to do
good unto all men. . . . And though for the present we seem to be
unsensible of the law and the law giver, yet when death and the Law
assault us, if we have our advocate to seek, who shall plead for us in
this case of conscience betwixt God and our own souls. . . .
   The law of love, peace and liberty in the states [extends] to Jews,
Turks, and Egyptians, as they are considered the sons of Adam,
which is the glory of the outward state of Holland. So love, peace and
liberty, extending to all in Christ Jesus, condemns hatred, war and
bondage. . . . Our desire is not to offend one of his little ones, in
whatsoever form, name, or title he appears in, whether Presbyterian,
Independent, Baptist, or Quaker, but shall be glad to see anything of
God in any of them, desiring to do unto all men as we desire all men
should to unto us, which is the true law both of Church and state. . . .
   Therefore if any of these said persons come in love unto us, we
cannot in conscience lay violent hands upon them, but give them free
egress and regress into our town and houses, as God shall persuade
our consciences. . . .

   Only the residents of today's Flushing, in Queens, appear to
commemorate the eloquence of the town's founders and to ren-
der tribute to the writers of one of the earliest statements on religious liberty of such broad character in all of the colonies.[19]

   Stuyvesant's response was quick and expected. He arrested the
sheriff of Flushing who bore the remonstrance to him and dismissed him from office. A few years later, he arrested and banished one of the Quakers, John Bowne, who promptly went to
Amsterdam to plead his case. After much deliberation, the Am-

sterdam Chamber sent Stuyvesant another reminder of the practical value of religious toleration:

> . . . although we heartily desire, that these and other sectarians re-
> mained away from there, yet as they do not, we doubt very much
> whether we can proceed against them rigourously without diminish-
> ing the population and stopping immigration, which must be favored
> at a so tender stage of the country's existence. You may therefore shut
> your eyes, at least not force people's consciences, but allow everyone
> to have his own belief, as long as he behaves quietly and legally,
> gives no offence to his neighbors and does not oppose the govern-
> ment. As the government of this city has always practised this maxim
> of moderation and consequently has often had a considerable influx of
> people, we do not doubt that your Province too would be benefitted
> by it.[20]

The "maxim of moderation" became the practice of English
New York, as well, not because policy so dictated but because
circumstances compelled it. The assumption of English control
did not homogenize the colony's religious complexion. "There
are religions of all sorts," complained Governor Andros in 1678.
A few years later, another governor was more caustic: he found
13 denominations in the province, "in short of all sorts of opinions there are some," but for the most part, there were "none at
all."[21] In Pennsylvania and New Jersey, the absence of an established church reflected the intention of their founders; in New
York, the indeterminate character of the Anglican Church developed from the complexity of the colony's population. The first
proprietor, the Duke of York, granted religious toleration as a
recognition of this diversity and of the need to pursue moderate
policies if trade and profits were to be promoted. In any case,
the Articles of Capitulation by which the Dutch surrendered
specified that the Reformed Church should remain undisturbed.
The first English governor, Richard Nicolls, went further, providing that the majority of the population in any town could establish a public church but that other congregations should be permitted to conduct their own services.[22] The prescription was repeated to Andros after the reacquisition of the province from

the Dutch in 1674 and was incorporated in the Charter of Liberties drawn up in 1683.[23]

The Glorious Revolution, which advanced the cause of religion in England by the Toleration Act, actually represented a backward step for New York. The province had already gone beyond the notion of one public church and second-class concessions to Dissenters. New Yorkers had come to see "the necessity of leaving religion to each man's conscience in the interest of getting on."[24] The feeble effort during the remainder of the colonial period to elevate the Anglican Church in status proved a failure. A Ministry Act of 1693 provided for public support of "a good sufficient Protestant Minister" in the four lower counties, but this is as close as the colony ever got to a church establishment; and the effort to interpret the law as an exclusive benefit to the Anglican Church was vigorously opposed by New York's many Dissenters. If the law of 1693 established any church, as Clinton Rossiter observed facetiously, "no one was quite sure what church it was."[25]

What developed in the province of New York was neither a clear separation of church and state nor a well-defined state church. In communities where non-Anglicans were in a majority, the proceeds of the Ministry Act could be used to support dissenting churches; in New York City, where the diversity of religions was most pronounced, the principle of voluntarism was followed. Ministers of the Anglican and Dutch churches continued to lament the "spirit of confusion" that resulted from New York's "perfect freedom of conscience," where everybody could "do what seems right in his own eyes, so long as he does not disturb the public peace."[26] New York's churchgoers were always more latitudinarian than their ministers. They were not strict in keeping the Sabbath, as one dismayed Bostonian discovered in 1704; and among the Dutch, even in Albany, where the domines ministered to a population that was largely Dutch, there was very little religion, as another visitor noted in 1744, and "not a grain" of enthusiasm.[27] Some New Yorkers saw virtue in the colony's confusion of religious voices: "the Variety of Sects" in the province was "a Guard against the Tyranny and Usurpation of one over another." Even the Deists, it was claimed, served a useful purpose by forcing casual Christians to re-examine the tenets of their own faith.[28]

Well before the Great Awakening constrained other colonists to recognize the danger of church establishments to their own new programs of spiritual regeneration, well before Isaac Backus and the Separatist Baptists preached the cause of religious voluntarism, and years before Jefferson expressed his fear of the danger to civil peace of state control of religion, New Yorkers had learned in the crucible of day-to-day living in a multifarious society the value of a neutral state which permitted creeds to compete for the spiritual affection of the citizenry. In New York, competition had strengthened freedom, not atheism; and the "natural right" of religious liberty was supported not by political theory so much as by long experience.[29]

Prejudice and mutual religious suspicions were not exorcised by the New York accommodation. Germans and Dutch eyed each other with distrust in the Mohawk Valley as did Presbyterians and Anglicans in New York City, but the state was not expected to create love, only harmony. Its role was neither to force its own orthodoxy on others nor to allow any denomination to try to do so. Its jurisdiction in religious matters was legitimate, as one of the colony's most vigorous polemicists put it, only when denominational opinion was converted into "Actions prejudicial to the Community," and then it was not the opinion but the action which was punishable.[30] New York entered the republic with a model to offer its neighbors which gave the lie to the sectarian argument that diversity bred only religious strife and immorality.

Tolerance in New York, as in the other colonies and in the future United States, had its limits; and the outer edge was passed where blacks were concerned. If racial violence is as American as cherry pie, then New York was typically American in this ugly respect, too, setting an example by its harsh repression of blacks suspected of crimes that were magnified in the public mind largely by the color of the perpetrators. Slavery in New York was more humane under the Dutch than under the English, resulting from a peculiar practice of granting some Negroes half-freedom as well as freedom, while others were held in bondage. No clear institutionalization of slavery could be developed amid such confusion; and none was.[31] Under the English, slavery expanded so that there were more bondsmen in New York than in any other northern colony; and one of the concomitants of the increase was the most severe violence against Negroes of any of the colonies. In 1712, 19 blacks were executed after an uprising in which about two dozen fired a building and killed five whites. The reprisals were grisly; the forms of execution included burning, starvation, and use of the medieval wheel. In 1741, a far more imaginary plot resulted in a witch hunt comparable in blind savagery to that at Salem a half-century earlier. The reprisals this time included 18 Negroes hanged, 13 burned at the stake, and 71 deported.[32]

What is prototypical about the racial violence is not so much the severity of the punishment as the confusion of the white population. It had learned cosmopolitanism as a way of life but had never fitted the black man into this scheme of accommodation. Unwilling or unable to enlarge their vision of diversity beyond the color line, white New Yorkers responded with a rationale that was to become more familiar in the succeeding century: the colony's slaves were treated with "great indulgence" and were better cared for than were the poor in Europe; those who had participated in the "villainous plot" were exceptional, and their "senseless" and "wicked enterprise" must be attributable to their seduction by the Devil.[33] Even in the twentieth century, northern, urban cosmopolitanism proved to be no guarantor of color blindness. Indeed, race prejudice was to become worse in the very centers of ethnic diversity which bred tolerance for whites. Colonial New York mirrored the national disease.

On the more favorable side, New York's slaves were employed not in gangs on great estates but in a variety of crafts, trades, and domestic service, ameliorating their lot to that extent and providing them with skills for freedom.[34] And the colony appears to have produced America's earliest black poet, one Jupiter Hammon, whose first work appeared in 1760 but whose name and verse disappeared thereafter from the pages of our color-con-scious histories.[35] Colonial New York's failure, like that of other colonies, was not that it neglected to cultivate the talents of its black men and women but that it made no provision for employ-ing those talents after slavery ended.

III

To pursue in similar detail other evidences of New York's proto-typicality in the American colonies would go beyond the con-fines of an essay intended to be no more than suggestive. The illustrations are numerous enough to provide grist for many doc-toral mills. New York, it is said today, is not the United States; yet many Europeans think it is. So in the eighteenth century, some-how New York conveyed the impression of its typicality. The city's shipping was well below that of the other colonial sea-ports, but Peter Kalm, the Swedish naturalist, visiting in 1750, was sure that New York's commerce was more extensive than that of any other place in British North America. New York was not the largest city in the colonies in the 1760's—Philadel-phia exceeded it by 5,000—but the visiting Lord Adam Gordon was surprised to discover the fact on his arrival. The city of New York, he commented, had "long been held at home, the first in America."[36] When that adopted American, Crevecoeur, raised the question of what an American was, the answer he gave in a nation still almost three-quarters English was that "they are a mixture of English, Scotch, Irish, French, Dutch, German, and Swedes."[37] From his observation post in Orange County, New York, he had made of the "new man" he saw in that colony the larger American. The misimpressions may have been the result of sheer ignorance, but it is curious how already New York was taken to be the image of greater America.

Colonial New York can boast of its firsts: the first school sup-ported by public funds, although under church control, and now the oldest private school in the country with a continuous exis-tence (the Collegiate School in New York City); the first chamber of commerce not organized under governmental auspices; the first play to be written and printed in America—the farce, *Androborus,* written by Governor Robert Hunter and presented in 1714; the first licensing of doctors, in New York City in 1760; the first legislative proceedings to be printed in any of the colonies, in 1695, at least 15 years before any of its neighbors followed suit;[38] as well as the enrichment of American popular culture by such Dutch innovations as Santa Claus, New Year's Eve celebrations, tenpin bowling; words such as "skipper," "sloop," and "yacht"; culinary delights like crullers and cookies and waffles; political terms like "boss" and "boodle"; and inimitable place names like Brooklyn, Harlem, and the Catskills.

Apart from its boost to local pride, firsts are probably of less significance than New York's seconds—or thirds. When the province did not lead, it was not very far behind. Culture was not New York's forte, since the "Art of getting Money" seemed to be the provincial preoccupation and, as Cadwallader Colden viewed it, "the only principle of life propagated among the young People"; but a corps of the province's young intellectuals tried hard in the mid-eighteenth century to compensate for the defect. Philadelphia organized its first philosophical society in 1743; five years later, New York City had a "Society for the Promotion of Useful Knowledge." In 1731, the Quaker City organized a public library; three years later, the Corporation of New York City was operating one with a librarian paid out of public monies (the salary was £3 a year but was raised to £4 after three years). The Philadelphians established the colonies' first hospital; New York was responsible for the second. The first medical school was opened in Philadelphia in 1765; New York began the second within three years. Boston had an informal medical society in 1736; New York followed, even if 13 years later. The Bay City had a legal discussion group operating in 1765; New York had a larger, better-organized, and more professional one—the Moot—five years later.[39] New Yorkers were rarely in the van, but their cultural aspirations always exceeded their grasp. When the New York Society Library was organized in 1754, the elaborate bookplate prepared for its volumes depicted New York City as the Athens of America!

New York's evening schools were not the only ones in the colonies, but by the Revolution the province had more of them than any of its neighbors. Philadelphia's Academy (later College) was the first institution of higher education in the colonies that was strictly secular in purpose and character; but when King's College was founded in 1754, a group of New York's intellectuals fought hard to make that province's equally secular. The effort failed, but the arguments for state control of education advanced in that controversy inspired the post-Revolutionary creation of the University of the State of New York, a model followed by other states similarly committed to the proposition that the supervision of education was the proper business of the public.[40]

New York's press was not as numerous as those of either Massachusetts or Pennsylvania—although not far behind; but in the 22 newspapers published at one time or another between 1725 and 1776 appeared some of the most lively and contentious political literature of all the colonial presses. Withal, the literary output of the Middle Colonies exhibited the kind of balance to which Turner had alluded. Of the South's literary productions during the period 1638–1783, more than half comprised statutes, laws, and executive proclamations. New England's output during this same period was preponderantly theological. The press of the Middle Colonies shows a remarkable balance of interests among the fields of politics, law, theology, education, social science, and literature.[41] If this analysis represents accurately the intellectual interests of the three sections, the Middle Colonies were truly the mediators between the two outer extremes.

The shape of the colonial economy of the Middle Atlantic region has yet to be drawn accurately, but even by rough and ready yardsticks, it was more varied, more stable, and less dependent upon single staples or industries than either of the other two regions. Agriculture in New York, as in Pennsylvania, was not a supplementary activity wrung from a barren soil to assist in supporting a trading population but was rather interlaced with trade, New York City providing the outlet for the products of the colony's farms. New York's paper money was better managed and less inflated than the currency of any of the colonies for which adequate statistics are available. The trade of the Middle Colonies reflects the mediating character of which Turner had written. In contrast with the South's dominantly bilateral and New England's heavily triangular trade patterns, the commerce of the middle region was partly triangular but more largely direct with Europe.[42] Conceivably, this was at the root of the region's prosperity on the eve of the Revolution and explains its hesitation in drawing the sword against England.

The French and Indian War provided New York with the largest boost to its economy, headquartering the British Army as it did, but the war points up even more the strategic and diplomatic significance of New York in the colonial and imperial structure. When Herbert L. Osgood wrote his four-volume *American Colonies in the Eighteenth Century*, he felt compelled to apologize in the preface for the extensive treatment given to New York. But, he explained, the four volumes dealt heavily with the Anglo-French Wars and, "of course, in all military relations in which Canada was involved New York was the strategic centre of the colonial territory. In a period of wars, therefore, it necessarily holds a prominent place, while in all that pertained to Indian relations its position was a leading one."[43] "Of course," indeed! What is surprising in Osgood's volumes is not the attention paid to New York but the need of an explanation for doing so. New York *was* the pivot of empire. It was the only colony in which British regular troops were stationed throughout virtually the entire colonial period. The four independent companies were woefully neglected, it is true, but their mere presence was symbolic of Whitehall's recognition of the strategic importance of New York and of its alliance with the Iroquois.[44] It was on the New York frontier that the rivalry between France and England was pursued most enduringly during the eighteenth century; and it was from New York's militant imperialists—Robert Livingston, Cadwallader Colden, Alexander Kennedy, James Alexander, William Livingston, and William Smith—that Britain received the most repeated suggestions for strengthening the empire and turning it to the mutual benefit of colonies and mother country.

It was in New York, significantly, that the most serious attempt to produce a colonial union was made; and the interest of both the colony's leaders and British officials was prompted by their recognition of the crucial role which New York, its Indian connections, and its fur trade bore in the imperial framework. And it was in New York, as the strategic center of empire, that the British Post Office in North America established its headquarters and to which it organized its packet service from England, in 1755, in order to provide the Crown with "early and frequent intelligence" of what was "in agitation" in its American colonies.[45]

Finally, there is politics, which in New York almost defies comprehension in the colonial period as it does today. The nature of New York's political structure and the mechanisms by which it operated are still being debated; but a number of conclusions seem acceptable even to the most contentious historians. There was no simple oligarchy of home-grown aristocrats; no politically mute masses; no clearly discernible clash between democrats and aristocrats, conservatives and radicals. What emerges is a complex, dynamic, and, in part, sophisticated preformation of the later political scene. Political factions reflected the heterogeneity of the colony's economy, its ethnic and religious composition, its geographic sectionalism, and its social structure. Parties were broad coalitions, and programs were necessarily diffuse enough to appeal to the colony's cosmopolitan population, often in a variety of languages. If there was deference, there was also democracy. If there was aristocracy, there was also public accountability. If there were family rivalries, there were also popular issues. If there were local concerns, there were also Anglo-American interests. If there was social stratification and monopoly of officeholding, there was also mobility and considerable rotation in office. If there was Whig ideology imported from England, there was also the uniquely American idiom in which it was couched by provincial politicians to suit the colony's special political dynamic. If the articulate were spokesmen of conservatism and status, there were also inarticulate believers in liberty and equality.

Even before the returns are in and while the historians still debate, one may hazard the proposition that the infrastructure of New York's politics was far more complex and interesting than its superstructure, and that the intensity of dialogue disclosed in the polemical literature flowing from the New York presses did not camouflage a mere shadow system of politicking. There surely must have been a contest over who should rule at home, but we are not yet certain who the contestants were or just what they wanted or whether they were always the same people or were consistent in their objectives. Somehow, New Yorkers learned during the colonial period to play the game of politics in the style which conditions dictated that later America should play it and which a future America came to expect. Somehow, its inhabitants learned to be, as a confused Henry Adams put it, "democratic by instinct" despite the colony's aristocratic tone. Perhaps the clue is provided by J. H. Plumb's astute observation concerning eighteenth-century English politics, that it was "always richer, freer, more open than the oligarchical nature of its institutions might lead one to believe." In those days neither suffrage nor even elections were at the heart of politics, Plumb says, but rather decision-making and "the turmoil they aroused" and the steady growth of "political consciousness."[46]

New York's colonial experience validates the conclusion perfectly. By 1775, New Yorkers were accustomed to what the country became so adept in during the years ahead. Only a non-New Yorker could be astonished to hear in New York City, on the eve of the Revolution, nothing but "Politics, politics, politics! . . . Men, women, children, all ranks and professions mad with Politics."[47]

When an English visitor in 1800 said of the Middle States that they seemed "never out of step in the national march," always about to become or being what the rest of the country was, he cast the region in its proper role. The role had already been played out while the states were still colonies. As for New York, that amateur historian, Theodore Roosevelt, may have been more perspicacious than he intended when he wrote in his little history of New York in 1891: "The most important lesson taught by the history of New York City is the lesson of Americanism."[48]

Local Government in Colonial New York: A Base for Republicanism

Patricia U. Bonomi

I

In 1957, Edmund Morgan observed in an influential article that for the previous 50 years colonial historians had been concentrating so closely on either the imperial or the economic and social aspects of early American history that they were neglecting the study of local institutions. Professor Morgan pointed to the need for investigating local land and tax patterns, the churches, schools, and clubs, the county courts, towns, and other units of local government, and "social groupings in every colony." It was in the examination of local experience, he suggested, that historians might observe the development of unique social attitudes and political practices that would eventually turn Englishmen into Americans. "No American," Morgan noted, "ever sat on the Board of Trade or the Privy Council. Few Americans ever came in contact with imperial officers. It was in local American institutions that these men gained their political experience."[1]

Much has happened in the field of early American history since 1957. The return to the study of local institutions that was already under way has accelerated sharply. Scholars trained in the social sciences have turned the study of American colonial history—once considered a rather rarefied pursuit—into a lively and creative experience. But now a new problem can be discerned. These recent studies have tended to focus mainly on that area which always seems to get an inordinate share of attention

—the New England colonies. There have been in-depth studies
of such towns as Dedham, Andover, Sudbury, Hingham, and
Plymouth.[2] Sufficient material has been gathered about the social
and political patterns of this section that scholars have begun to
construct new syntheses, Michael Zuckerman's recent study of
New England towns being an outstanding example.[3] If we skip
over the Middle Colonies and look at the South (which is exactly what historians usually do) it becomes evident that in the
southern colonies too some attention has been directed to local
institutions—at least to those of a political nature. One thinks
first of Charles Sydnor's elegant little book about Washington's
Virginia, and then of the Browns' study of that same colony, together with a few scattered others.[4]

But what of the Middle Colonies? What about Pennsylvania,
New Jersey, and New York, whose cultural diversity and spirited
politics would seem to be full of promise for scholars drawn to
the study of local institutions? Through the years some excellent
work has been done, though much of it has concentrated in
three areas: biographies, studies of the Quakers, and mono-
graphs on the politics of the Revolutionary Era. There are signs,
however, that a new interest in these colonies may be developing. Studies of early Pennsylvania politics, of Middle-Colony
land patterns, the legal profession in New York and New Jersey,
workingmen's organizations, and of Anglo-American politics in
New York have appeared in recent years.[5]

To date this reviving interest has not to my knowledge produced any detailed studies of local government—a subject that
took first priority for students of both New England and the
South. And there is a reason for this lack. Everyone knows that
the unit of local government in New England was the township,
and everyone also knows that local government in the South was
organized by counties and run by the County Courts. But do we
really have more than a hazy notion of how local government
was organized in the Middle Colonies? There were counties, of
course, but there were other jurisdictions too, and it is not always clear what these were or how they were governed.

Stone dwelling in Kingston, New York used as the first meeting place of the New York State Senate. *Photograph courtesy of The New York State Trust for Historic Preservation.*

II

Local government in New York—the focus of this essay—raises particular difficulties. We are always encountering those Hudson Valley land barons who are supposed to have exercised such control over local politics. But getting past the grandees is really a minor problem compared to that of figuring out exactly what the forms and jurisdictions of New York's local government were. Since I have dealt with this subject in some detail elsewhere, I shall give only the briefest outline of it here.

For most of the colonial period New York consisted of ten counties—five located along the seaboard and around the port of New York City, and five in the Hudson Valley bordering the river. These counties in turn were subdivided either into townships or, in some cases, into units called precincts. Long Island had over a dozen and a half townships by the early eighteenth century; Westchester County had eight by the 1730's; and Ulster County, on the west bank of the Hudson, had at least five townships by the same period. In the more sparsely settled sections of the province, precincts were established. These initially encompassed fairly large areas, but as population increased they were gradually subdivided into smaller units. Dutchess County, on the east bank of the river, included seven precincts by 1737; and Orange County, on the west bank, had at least five. When these counties were first established in 1691, it was expected that in accordance with English forms Justices of the Peace, sitting as County Courts, would govern them. By 1703, however, a new system had evolved. County Boards of Supervisors, composed of men elected annually from each of the subcounty jurisdictions, had taken over from the County Courts all responsibilities for the collection and disbursement of tax monies, in most areas leaving the County Courts with an exclusively judicial responsibility. This alteration in the form of county government was of no small importance, for it meant that a large degree of power was thereby shifted from an appointive to an elective body.

Townships in New York were governed by a board of from six to twelve trustees, elected every year by the "inhabitants and freeholders" of each township at their annual meetings. The precincts also held annual meetings at which were elected one supervisor, together with assessors, constables, fence viewers, and other officers as needed. And where do the manors—those vast landholdings of which we hear so much in the pages of New York history—fit into this scheme? Contrary to original expectations, manor government followed a form similar to that already outlined. Manors either joined with the surrounding area to form a township or precinct, or composed such a unit in themselves. Thus manor residents also had the privilege of electing supervisors, assessors, constables, town clerks, and other local officers. That the opinions of manor proprietors may have received special consideration from local officials is quite likely, but this does not necessarily mean that the landed grandees "controlled" local government. It was not unusual for manor proprietors to object to the way they were treated by local governments, as, for example, in 1722 when the Livingston family believed that local assessors had set too high a tax quota for Livingston Manor. But they decided it was useless to protest since, in the words of Philip Livingston, the assessors "will do what they please."[6]

One other unit of local government in New York—the chartered city—should be mentioned. There were two of these in the province—New York City and Albany. Under their English charters, formally granted in 1686, the governor appointed for each city a mayor, recorder, clerk, and weighers and measurers. The electors annually chose an alderman and an assistant from each ward, and assessors, collectors, and constables as needed. After 1731, for example, the citizens of New York City elected 14 aldermen and assistants, 7 assessors, and 16 constables each year.[7]

This, then, in brief outline is the general picture of local government in New York Colony. Its major components were counties, towns, precincts, and chartered cities. For a more immediate sense of how local government actually worked and of how it affected the lives and the political perceptions of the colonists, I decided for the present purpose to focus on a single community, the Township of Kingston, in Ulster County on the west bank of the Hudson River. The reasons for choosing Kingston are several. First, it provides an opportunity to examine how ordinary citizens of New York related to their local government, as Ulster was on the whole a county of small farms and small towns and villages. There were some large tracts in Ulster, but these were located on the county's western frontier; they remained largely undeveloped during the colonial era, and thus they did not markedly alter the dominant pattern of small holdings. Second, Kingston was an important Hudson River town and entrepôt. Indeed, it was one of the oldest in the colony, having been established originally as a Dutch fur trading post. Thus it developed a commercial as well as an agrarian character, as was the case with many other New York towns located along the water. Another reason for this choice was that sufficient records of early Kingston have been preserved to make possible at least a partial reconstruction of seventeenth- and eighteenth-century ways. There are Grand Jury lists, assessment records, deeds and wills, a few lists of freeholders, and even some of the minutes of the Board of Trustees.

By drawing together information from these various sources, I found it possible to construct a list of 135 men who served on the Kingston Board of Trustees from 1711 until the Revolution. (See Appendix, p. 118). After each name are shown the years served on the Board, the occupation when obtainable, the county offices in which the individual served, and the amount he was assessed in various years. Of particular interest are the occupations of the trustees. Few were gentlemen; most seem to have been of the middling sort. Many were farmers, but a surprisingly large number were artisans. Of those whose occupations are known, four were gentlemen, eight merchants, one a doctor, one a schoolmaster, twenty-seven were farmers or yeomen, and fifty were artisans. Of the artisans there were ten shoemakers, nine in the carpentry trades, six blacksmiths, five tailors, four brewers, four weavers, plus a scattering of coopers and masoners, and one was a barber. I have so far been unable to determine the occupations of forty-four men.

The length of time that men served on the Board appears to have varied sharply. The two extremes are perhaps of greatest interest here. Jan Post served only in 1711, possibly because he moved on to the position of Supervisor in 1712. Johannis Hardenbergh, Henry Beekman, Jr., Gilbert Livingston, and Abraham Hasbrouck also served one or, at most, two years, but they were men of wealth and influence whose public service was usually rendered at a higher level of government. Aldert Roosa served only one year, but he moved to the neighboring town of Hurley; and Nicholas Demeyer and Jan Plough, whose assessments rose rapidly, may have decided that public service took too much time from their occupations. Arie Van Vliet appears to have had something of a struggle, and since it took him 23 years to rise from ordinary corporal to 3rd corporal of the militia, he may simply have been one of those honest nonentities whose limits were generally perceived soon after his first public exposure. Several individuals, on the other hand, served from 10 to 20 years on the Board. Some went on to higher county positions, but others appear to have gone no further in public service. Several families are strongly represented: five members of the Wynkoop family served a total of 50 years in the period from 1711 to 1776; five Elmendorphs served 28 years, five Jansens 43, four Ten Broecks 33, and seven Slechts served a total of 58 years.

The frequency with which certain family names appear on the roll of trustees raises the question of whether a few families may have dominated Kingston government as a sort of local elite. It is undoubtedly true that over time certain families were more prominent than others, but there is no indication that this set very sharp limits on infusions of new blood. Members of 64 different families served as trustees in the years 1711 to 1776. Moreover, an interesting fact emerges from a comparison of the list of trustees with a list of freeholders that was compiled in 1728. This shows that of the 148 freeholders living at Kingston in 1728, 61—or over 41 percent of the total—served at some time during their lives as trustees.[8] The Board of Trustees, it would seem, was hardly an exclusive fraternity. One does note that the number of men serving consecutive terms—sometimes as many as a dozen years in a row—increased from the 1730's on. This would seem to reflect the growing stability of the town as it lost many frontier characteristics. Moreover, newcomers had to establish themselves as solid members of the community before they could hope for election to the Board. Most trustees after the 1730's were second-generation Kingstonians.

The genealogical material tells us something about the ages of the trustees. In the decade from 1711 to 1720, the average age of newly elected trustees was 32. This rose to the late 30's in the period 1721 through 1760, and rose again to an average of around 42 years in the decade and a half before the Revolution. Again, this can probably be read as a sign of the community's more settled character as the eighteenth century progressed. It might be noted, however, that throughout the colonial period the average age of Kingston trustees at first election was lower than that of selectmen in Dedham and Watertown, Massachusetts, which has been calculated at an average of 45 years.[9]

This chart, with its information about the economic, family, and political background of the Kingston trustees, reveals certain things of interest about community life in that eighteenth-century town. Yet anyone who has ever engaged in this sort of information-collecting knows that it has its limits. Though it does help to establish a base of facts and statistics, it cannot reveal how men *felt* about their public duties. One wants to know more about the quality of local officeholding, about the kinds of responsibilities involved, and about the interaction between officeholders and the citizenry of the province. And one wants to know more about the broader political context. As Edmund Morgan and others have asked, how did this local political experience affect the colonists' attitudes toward government and authority; how did it shape political expectations? One way to gain some understanding of the special qualities—if indeed they were special—of local politics in the colonies, is to view them against the background of local practices in England. If Americans—in this case, New Yorkers—were being affected in unique ways by their experiences, if they were developing new modes of political behavior, the patterns of the two societies should manifest various points of divergence.

III

If local government in New York seems complex, that of Old England appears almost chaotic. The major jurisdictions, always tangled and overlapping, include counties, hundreds, boroughs, manors, townships, and parishes. By the end of the seventeenth century, a degree of order had found its way into the system. At the top level of local government were the counties, and these were run by the County Courts, mainly through their Quarter Sessions. All top county officers—the Justices of the Peace, Lords Lieutenants, sheriffs, and others—were appointed and, traditionally, these posts went to members of the local gentry. It is clear that county government in New York broke sharply from the English model when elected Boards of Supervisors took over most of the nonjudicial duties of the County Courts. Still, the Justices of the Peace retained jurisdiction in many important civil and criminal matters, and it is perhaps worth pausing a moment to take a look at the sort of persons who filled those posts in New York. P. M. G. Harris, in a recent study of "The Social Origins of American Leaders," includes Justices of the Peace as members of the colonial "upper class" almost as a matter of course.[10] This may be valid for some colonies—Sydnor believed that the County Courts in Virginia were the preserve of the gentry. But the picture is not quite so clear in New York. There, many Justices of the Peace were not of the top layer of provincial society. Those offices were by no means filled exclusively from the ranks of the wealthy landholders, merchants, and lawyers who formed the colonial elite. A glance at the chart shows that while some Justices of the Peace would qualify as patricians—for example, Henry Beekman and Johannis Hardenbergh—others were solidly middle-class. Take a few examples: Evert Wynkoop was from a family of brewers and shoemakers, prosperous but not wealthy; Mattyse Janse, a shoemaker all his life, left only a moderate estate, including from £20 to £35 to each of six children; Cornelius DeLametter came from a family of artisans and local officeholders; his brother Johannis, also a Justice of the Peace, was a shoemaker. Of the 21 Justices of the Peace listed in this

chart, only seven might qualify as members of the Ulster County
elite. The others gained their livelihoods by their own hands in
such occupations as farmer, brewer, and shoemaker. But then
how could it be otherwise in a land where there was no native
gentry but many jobs to fill?

Looking at the subcounty levels of English local government
for possible models of comparison with our Township of Kingston, we might turn to either the English parish or the manor.
Taking the manor first, we find authorities agreeing that during
the eighteenth century many manors gave over most of their
governing responsibilities to either the parishes or to nearby boroughs.[11] In the rural areas the parish became the key local governing unit, mainly because it gained from the manor the power
to tax the local inhabitants.[12] For this reason, the English parish
may offer the closest parallel to the colonial township of the
eighteenth century. There were from 8,000 to 10,000 parishes in
England, and these were, according to the Webbs, the most immediate governing authority for five-sixths of the English population.[13] At the top of parish government were from two to four
churchwardens and a vestry consisting of one to two dozen men.
Other officers such as petty constables, surveyors of highways,
and overseers of the poor were appointed for each parish by the
County Courts. The churchwardens were chosen either by the
incumbents or by the vestry as a whole, though sometimes the
parishioners elected them, and in a few cases they were appointed by a manor lord. The vestry seems in most cases to have
been a self-perpetuating body, with new members being chosen
by cooptation. All authorities agree that the churchwardens and
vestrymen were generally the "principal" or "chiefest" and "most
substantial" men in the community.[14]

Because these offices were unsalaried, they were filled mainly
by local leaders and rate payers—the resident squire, the more
substantial yeomen, the miller, and perhaps the innkeeper. In
the larger and more powerful parishes, men of higher rank were
prominent. This was especially true in the regions of London,
Westminster, and Bristol, and in the northern counties. The
Webbs note, for example, that by general understanding the ves-

try of St. James, Piccadilly, was composed of one-third noblemen, one-third gentlemen and Members of Parliament, and one-third businessmen—and they find the same formula used in some other areas.[15]

The parish officers were obligated to hold an open meeting, sometimes called a Town Meeting, with the inhabitants each year around Easter time. There is evidence that in some places, at certain periods, such open meetings took place more often than once a year, and that the townspeople participated quite directly in the vestry business of setting tax rates and passing local ordinances. A more common form, however, seems to have been the closed or "select" vestry, which made little effort to gain popular consent for its actions and, as the Webbs note, to the "poorer folk" must have "appeared an uncontrollable parish oligarchy." Nor are the Webbs alone in this estimate. W. E. Tate, whose detailed investigation of parish records was first published in 1946 in his book *The Parish Chest*, concludes that "aristocracy, plutocracy, or oligarchy, not pure democracy, was the fundamental basis of the parochial organisation."[16] Additional confirming evidence comes from Sumner Chilton Powell, who looked into local government in Weyhill parish and manor, Hampshire, to establish background for his book *Puritan Village*. Powell does not depict Weyhill as having a completely oligarchic system, but he does see a conservative village, steeped in the traditions of a feudal past, that was loath to change the habits of centuries. All land was rented from the manor; the court baron, which was held once a year, dealt largely with petty misdemeanors and was "not a meeting of villagers to discuss new ways of solving social problems." As for the Weyhill parish meetings, these were "dull affairs, attended by only a handful of men who merely went through perfunctory motions."[17]

One other unit of English local government seems to have shared certain characteristics with such a place as Kingston, New York: the English borough. Kingston, by the second quarter of the eighteenth century, had added a commercial side to its earlier agrarian character. And historians have sometimes noted that in the more commercial centers of England men might rise quite swiftly from ordinary beginnings to positions of power and prestige. The English borough town was governed by a mayor, aldermen, and burgesses, usually from 12 to 24 men. Sometimes these leaders were elected by the people at large, but more often the choice was made by only the leading freemen of the borough, with the result that government fell into the hands of a few men. Powell notes that in the borough of Sudbury, in Suffolk, government was conducted "quite apart from the commoners," and "in fact, to question the mayor was a criminal offense."[18] Borough officers were not paid, and in larger towns their duties often became so onerous that the eligibles grew apathetic about local government. This was shown in their efforts to avoid public office. Those who could afford it sometimes hired substitutes, but because these proxies were often men of mean degree—small professionals and tradesmen—they have frequently been blamed for the decline of eighteenth-century municipal government noted by many English historians. In some areas borough government fell into such disrepute that parish officers resumed control. Elsewhere Justices of the Peace took over. The latter, often known as "trading justices," were notorious in some areas for their venal and corrupt practices.[19] J. H. Plumb may have overstated the case when he wrote that the corporate towns were dominated by "self-perpetuating oligarchs, utterly uninterested in social administration, who squandered and abused corporate wealth and corporate charities,"[20] but it cannot be doubted that the failure of such governments to meet their growing responsibilities and to correct abuses helped point up the need for the reorganization that was finally begun under the Municipal Reform Act of 1835.

Some of the most telling comments about seventeenth- and eighteenth-century local government in England are to be found elsewhere than in the history books. English literature of that period has a good deal to say about the men of less than gentle birth who managed to acquire some power in local government. Following the path of Shakespeare and others, a number of seventeenth-century writers made sport of local officeholders, with the constable serving as a favorite comic character. In the works of Middleton and Glapthorne, the constables "Blurt" and "Busie" are depicted as fools and braggarts, inflated with self-importance. But by the eighteenth century there is a noticeable change of tone in the literature, the local official being no longer the blundering but harmless creature of the earlier satires. Now he is a venal and malicious figure, whom we can no longer view with easy indulgence. Henry Fielding's Mr. Justice Thrasher, for example, is depicted as an opinionated and unfeeling bigot who decides cases solely on the grounds of his personal prejudices, and Smollett's Mr. Justice Gobble, a tailor who has risen above his station by marrying a rich widow, is brutal and vengeful, in no way a comic figure.[21] The changed literary imagery of the eighteenth century may well have reflected a growing disillusionment with English local government, with criticism and suspicion being directed particularly against officials of ordinary birth. Obviously many Englishmen still believed that only a man of wealth and "independence" could resist the temptations to bribery and chicanery that inevitably corrupted a man of lower rank. In America, the case could not be viewed in any such extreme way. There, the vast majority of provincial officeholders at all levels of government had come from other than aristocratic origins.

IV

Against this background, let us turn again to New York and look more closely at the activities of the Kingston Board of Trustees. Fortunately some of the Board's minutes have survived, including the full record for the years 1714 through 1736. From this record emerges unmistakably the picture of a vigorous and active body engaged in making decisions important to the citizens of Kingston in their daily comings and goings.

The Kingston Board of Trustees consisted of 12 members—a larger number than sat on the Boards of Selectmen in most New England towns. In view of the difficulty in getting such a large number of persons to attend meetings regularly, it might be suspected that the Board's powers fell by default to a few active members. But not, it seems, at Kingston. The trustees themselves took steps to prevent this by ruling that members be required to attend meetings on penalty of a three shilling fine; they even fined members from one to three shillings for arriving late. In the years for which a complete set of minutes exist, meetings were attended by an average of ten trustees—quite a remarkable record. The Board met formally on an average of seven to nine times a year, though there seem to have been other informal meetings for the purpose of laying out town lots. Meetings were concentrated in the months of February, March, April, and May. On several occasions the trustees met four times within a 30-day period, and to assemble three times in one month was not unusual.[22]

The activities of the Board were varied, though easily the greatest part of its work had to do with the granting of land. The major sections of town land had been granted by the early eighteenth century, though one 60-acre farm was sold to Jan Post in 1713. Most of the plots mentioned in the Minutes, however, were for smaller town lots of about two acres, or for a few acres to tidy up the borders of someone's farm or pasture. In addition to supervising land allotments, the trustees also devoted much time to defending the town against claims for quit-rents, building local defenses and billeting soldiers in times of war, and paying town bills.[23] In 1736 they appropriated money for the building of a town dock, and in 1753 the trustees provided a generous quantity of rum to be distributed among the men assisting in the construction of a market house for the town. They levied fines on townsfolk who failed to clean their streets, carried lighted pipes after dark, rode through the town at more than a "moderate trot," or neglected to bury their dead cattle. The Board established rules for the admission of freemen (a £3 fee for a "Stranger" to set up trade), in 1728 set an 8 percent rate on money at interest, and in 1757 passed an ordinance restricting the movements after 9 P.M. of Negroes and slaves (of whom there were many in Kingston) on pain of whippings or fines.[24] As early as 1722 the Board of Trustees appropriated £30 for the maintenance of "a Dutch School Master,"[25] who was to keep a school that would be "Free for the Corporation Inhabitants."

At times the Board's activities were guided directly by the townspeople. Such was certainly the case at the annual town meetings on the first Tuesday in March, when, in addition to electing officers, the freeholders and freemen also voted on issues of importance. Kingston's charter provided that on petition of any three freeholders a town meeting could be assembled. Such may have been the initiative for the general town meeting called by the trustees in April 1725 to set the heights for fences within the corporation. At that meeting, the freeholders decided by majority vote to build their field fences 52 inches high, and to set lot fences at 5 feet. While they were meeting, they also passed rules providing that all fowls were to have one wing clipped, and that hogs should not be allowed to run in the streets.[26] Though such special town meetings did take place, there is no evidence that they were very frequent or that the meetings at Kingston played as important a civic role as did those of New England. Rather it was the Board of Trustees that constituted the locus of government in Kingston, with power being largely delegated by the people to the town's elected officials.[27]

There is abundant evidence throughout the records that the men elected to office took their responsibilities as a serious public trust. There is only one instance in the period from 1714 to 1736 of an elected trustee refusing to serve, and that case received such prominence in the record that it takes on the air of an exceptional situation. When Wessel Ten Broeck, elected a trustee on March 3, 1719, refused to accept the office, the new Board immediately ordered that he be fined 36 shillings and that he be prosecuted before the Justices of the Peace.[28] This case throws an additional bit of light on town elections. Mr. Evert Wynkoop, who had the next highest number of votes, came on the Board in Ten Broeck's place, indicating that more than 12 men had sought to become trustees in the March, 1719 election. The reluctance to serve in local office that was so pronounced in

England, though it crops up occasionally in New York, does not seem to have been a major theme. The willingness to serve extends even to such lesser local offices as those of assessor, constable, collector, highway commissioner, and fence viewer. Three men were elected in each of those categories every year. Many of them were incumbent, past, or future trustees, and a number of them were men of considerable property and status.[29]

Another point of interest concerns the attitude displayed by the Boards of Trustees toward the leading figures of the county. While the views of the local dons may well have carried special weight, there is nothing to suggest that the town fathers were easily cowed. Any challenge to the town's boundaries, for example, was sure to make the trustees bristle. For years the Board held out against the boundary claims of Johannis Hardenbergh and other patentees of the huge Hardenbergh Patent. Finally in 1746 the dispute had to be settled by arbitration. Nor was the Board intimidated when the incumbent Ulster County Assemblyman, Colonel Jacob Rutsen, insisted in 1726 that they pay over to him certain monies. The trustees flatly refused to pay on the ground that the charges were "Very Unreasonable." In 1727 the Board did not hesitate to put one Peek DeWitt "out of possession" of his town lands, presumably for nonpayment, even though the DeWitt family was a numerous and substantial one with a long history in the town.[30]

All in all the records of eighteenth-century Kingston reveal a fairly consistent pattern of strong and independent local government, with citizen participation coming from a broad spectrum of the community. There can be little doubt that many important decisions affecting the lives of the people of Kingston were in the hands of their locally elected officials—decisions regarding their lands, tax and interest rates, physical security, health, the education of their children, and their opportunities for economic advancement.

But though all this may have been true for Kingston, one might ask whether it also holds true for other parts of New York province, especially counties like Westchester and Dutchess where there were a number of large manors and patents, per-

haps imparting a more elitist quality to community life. In Westchester, it is no doubt true that the two large manors still existing in the eighteenth century, Philipsburgh and Cortlandt,* and
the smaller Manor of Morrisania, conferred a special influence
on the families that owned them. Certainly Philipses, Van Cortlandts, and Morrises were prominent at the provincial level of
government, and their influence was strong in parts of the county.
But it will be remembered that there were at least eight chartered towns, encompassing about half of the land, in Westchester; and surviving records have much to say about the strength
and independence of their local governments. Indeed, if direct
participation by its citizens is any measure of a town's political
vitality, such Westchester towns as Mamaroneck, Bedford, and
Rye would stand very high. There the town meeting was an active institution, owing perhaps to the New England origins of
the County's early settlers. The kinds of decisions made by the
Board of Trustees at Kingston—regarding land distribution, the
building of a mill, the admission of newcomers—were determined by majority vote of the town in a number of Westchester
communities. Moreover, the town minutes are replete with elections of townsmen to committees supervising everything from
the laying out of town lots to the drawing up of rules for the
impounding of stock.[31] Thus local government in Westchester
appears to be somewhat more complex than one might gather
from histories that stress only its aristocratic side.

Insofar as the three manors are concerned, both Cortlandt and
Morrisania had been weakened as jurisdictional entities in the
eighteenth century as they were being divided among family
members and land was being sold off. Philipsburgh, on the other
hand, retained its identity and boundaries, and there land continued to be leased rather than sold. What, then, was local government like at Philipsburgh? The few scattered records that remain reveal that the manor residents met together each April, at
what they termed "Town Meetings," to elect local officers and,
according to an entry for April 1, 1766, "to mak[e] town Laws for
that year."[32] The officers elected included assessors, constables,
collectors, pound masters, fence viewers, overseers of the roads,

a supervisor, and a town clerk—perhaps 20 elected officials each year. There was no Board of Trustees, nor is there any way of judging what sorts of rules were discussed at the annual town meetings. That the manor proprietor carried special weight within his bailiwick cannot be doubted, though the only time this is clearly evident in the existing town minutes is in 1773, when it was noted that a change of location for a road had been agreed to and "allowed" by Frederick Philipse.[33] Thus a mixed picture emerges from the Philipsburgh record. The manor tenants must have been aware at all times that they were under the watchful eye of their landlord, but to say that the Philipses "controlled" local affairs is to put the matter far too strongly. Indeed, insofar as the central issue of annual tax rates was concerned, the manor residents had the same rights as New Yorkers in other areas.

Dutchess and Albany counties also contained some large manors and patents, and there too the landlords enjoyed certain advantages. But because of factors I have examined elsewhere, having to do mainly with quarrels between members of the elite which forced them to cultivate the friendship and political support of the tenants, small farmers, and tradesmen in their counties, landlord influence again falls well short of "control."[34] True, there were no townships—only precincts—in Dutchess County, and the same holds for large areas of Albany County. Still, most of the adult males of those counties were eligible to participate each spring in annual elections and town meetings, where they chose officials who set and collected their taxes and performed other duties and services that had a direct impact on the life of the community.[35]

V

What, then, might we conclude about local government in colonial New York? What was its influence on the habits of the people at large, and what was its importance in shaping the political ideas that moved so swiftly to the front of the colonial consciousness in the Revolutionary Era? The first possibility is that New York local government was far more vigorous and independent than has heretofore been recognized. The pattern of energetic activity discerned at Kingston appears to be fairly representative of the other chartered towns and cities of the province, and almost 50 percent of the people lived within such jurisdictions. Moreover, those who did not live within chartered corporations still had the privilege of electing their supervisors, assessors, constables, and others, and many citizens served in local offices of greater or lesser degree. Perhaps more important is that officeholding in the colonies and officeholding in Old England were seen in very different lights. The key difference lay not in the form but in the substance of power. Local government in England was fenced about by tradition, often devoid of real power, and it offered limited scope for a man of imagination and initiative. To most ordinary Englishmen, officeholding was an obligation rather than an opportunity. The provincial concept of local government, on the other hand, seems to have been one of public trust, plus something more. One is struck, for example, by the case of Peter Noyes, a founding father of the town of Sudbury, Massachusetts. Noyes's offices, as listed by Sumner Chilton Powell, ranged from church elder, selectman, and judge of small causes, to town deputy to the provincial legislature. Over a 20-year span, he attended 129 official meetings in the town, and was "responsible for over six hundred and fifty separate 'orders,' carrying the weight of law and often the power of life and death over his townsmen."[36] Such a man as Johannis Jansen of Kingston, who served his town over 34 years in a comparable range of offices, must have compiled a record very much like that of Noyes. One could say of New York what Michael Zuckerman has said of New England: "Power did not descend mysteriously from above. Power was personal, and it could be seen close up."[37] And how could it be otherwise when, as noted earlier, there was no native gentry to draw on? The pool of patrician talent in America—the body of "real" gentlemen—was so small that most officials had to come from the general society. Even the "gentry" that did exist was a bootstrap gentry, and if, as seems likely, officeholding was itself one of the bootstraps, what the gentleman-officeholder represented was more a model to emulate than a personage to revere.

More than one historian has recognized that the most truly radical aspect of the American Revolution, and of the constitutions that were formulated in its wake, was the vesting of power in the people under a republican form of government. It *was* radical indeed, especially in view of the universal recognition by intellectuals of the eighteenth century that the republican state was among the most fragile then known. It was the deep awareness of this fragility, as John Howe has pointed out, that accounts for much of the ideological tension of the American Republic's earliest years.[38] Nonetheless the Americans did choose republicanism with virtual unanimity, and perhaps the extraordinary thing about this, as Gordon Wood has argued, "is the faith, not the doubts, of the Revolutionary leaders."[39] It is the faith— the taking for granted, we might say—that no other form of government comported nearly so well with the settled habits of the people, that needs explanation.

More than one royal governor complained that the provincial assemblies they had to deal with were hotbeds of republicanism, and it is quite correct to say that the colonies emerged at the very outset of the Revolution as 13 fully constituted self-governing republics. But self-government—government not simply by consent but by active, daily consent—begins not at the provincial but at the local level. Thus additional light on the habits and experience which served as a base for revolutionary republicanism may only be obtained, I am suggesting, by a far more general and systematic study of local government in the colonies than has hitherto been made.

Hannah Arendt, in comparing the American Revolution to those in other parts of the world, has perceived in a theoretical way the importance of local government as a source of popular sovereignty and political experience. Such a base of political competence was not present in France, for example, and Arendt describes the difficulties this caused as leaders struggled to build a stable republic—a struggle that included, as she notes, no fewer than 14 separate French constitutions between 1789 and 1875. As she says, "What was lacking in the Old World were the townships of the colonies. . . ."[40] Latin America offers endless examples of the difficulty of establishing republican states where the people have had little experience in self-government. The beginnings have often seemed auspicious, but with no solid underpinning upon which to build, power soon drifts back to the center and becomes lodged once more in the hands of its traditional custodians. Tocqueville himself noted the contribution that local government made to the success of the Revolution. "The American Revolution broke out, and the doctrine of the sovereignty of the people came out of the townships, and took possession of the State." But Tocqueville was talking about New England townships; he and many others have recognized the formative nature of the New England experience with local government. Was it, however, restricted to New England? Suppose that further investigation—which is very much needed for areas *outside* of New England—should reveal that in the Middle Colonies, or possibly even in the South, local government also showed extraordinary vitality? Here would be an important unifying element of the American experience, one that not only bound the 13 colonies together but also one that sets them off in sharper relief from revolutionary and republican experiments in other parts of the world.

There is, of course, a paradox in all this, since another name for what I have been discussing is parochialism. And parochialism, as we know only too well, has been a notorious theme in American culture—political culture and all other kinds. The town of Kingston, New York, judging from its written colonial remains, was nothing if not parochial. And yet in the methodical tenacity with which the citizens' elected officials dealt with so wide a variety of the town's daily concerns—many of them quaintly trivial—may be read a larger meaning. Should that parochialism be challenged from the outside, as it was here and in a thousand similar places in the 1770's, they would make a special point of insisting on their competence to do what they had in fact been doing all along—managing those affairs, trivial and otherwise, for themselves. In this setting, then, there was a sense

in which parochialism and republicanism—the essence of which
is government by consent—amounted to much the same thing.
And it may well have been this very parochialism—its very narrowness of view, its suspiciousness, its jealous attachment to
local prerogatives—that furnished the vital ingredient and much
of the staying power to the Americans' revolutionary and, later,
to their republican consciousness.

New York: Prototype of Modern America

Lawrence H. Leder

L ET ME BEGIN by announcing my complete sympathy with the thrust of both papers. I agree with Professor Bonomi's concern for a study of the impact of parochialism, her concern over the scholarly emphasis upon New England and the South and the paucity of Middle Colony studies, and her suggestion that the lack of research in local government was a major factor. Professor Klein postulates that New York's true importance lies in the fact that it is the prototype of modern America, and perhaps because of that very reason the colony's past has been slighted.

Although I agree with Professor Bonomi's conclusion, I cannot wholly accept her reasons for the lack of local government studies. She comments that "studies of local government . . . took first priority for students of both New England the South." Perhaps it is merely a problem of perspective. James Truslow Adams, Charles Francis Adams, Samuel Eliot Morison, Robert C. Winthrop, E. A. J. Johnson, G. L. Kittredge, George L. Haskins, Bernard Bailyn, Charles M. Andrews, Perry Miller, Kenneth Murdock, Edmund Morgan, and many others have made their reputations as New England historians and have written broad, thematic treatments of its past. These studies appeared on the scene well before the more specific (and perhaps more precise) studies of Kenneth Lockridge, Sumner Chilton Powell, John Waters, Philip Greven, and John Demos. Indeed, it is possible that the latter historians would have found difficulty in formulating the questions they asked without the knowledge provided by the vast framework of generalized studies which preceded their work. Much the same point can be made for the history of the southern colonies, going back to Philip A. Bruce, Thomas J.

Wertenbaker, B. C. Steiner, Newton Mereness, Percy Flippen, Louis B. Wright, and Wesley Frank Craven.

Professor Bonomi's cogent plea for a study of local institutions in the Middle Colonies, and particularly in New York, runs head-on into a problem which we are discussing right now. The resources of published works on which the scholar can rely for guidance and which can help him formulate meaningful questions for in-depth studies are extraordinarily limited. In 1956 an essay in *New York History* pointed up some research opportunities in the colony's eighteenth-century history, its neglected period from 1680 to 1750.[1] It followed on the heels of a significant essay on the same topic the year before by Frederick Tolles in the *William and Mary Quarterly*.[2]

Both essays emphasized the need for a revival of traditional approaches to history. As Professor Tolles put it, "The field shows no signs of being 'mined out'. . . . I am not convinced that we must resort to new mining techniques in order to maintain a profitable yield. I am all too conscious of the untapped veins that still remain to be opened, of the need to reassay some long-mined ores, to shore up some old shafts and relight them by the traditional lamps of conscientious historical investigation. . . . I am prepared to call the social scientists in as consulting engineers, to experiment with some of the 'new approaches' they have suggested. But I am not ready yet to turn the operation over to them."

Indeed, the approach which both essays emphasized, and which is particularly pertinent for New York, is biography. Professor Tolles called for "full-scale, full-bodied lives" of Cadwallader Colden, William Livingston, and governors Robert Hunter and William Burnet. (Let me hasten to add that a potentially fine biography of William Livingston has since been finished, but Professor Klein has not yet brought it into print; I hope that he soon will do so, for it is a significant work which should be more widely available.) The essay in *New York History* suggested additional New York figures, including Sir William Johnson, Abraham DePeyster, James Alexander, Peter Schuyler, George Clarke, Samuel Mulford, and William Smith. Of all these names,

Edward Hyde, Lord Cornbury, Governor of New York, 1701–1708, in female attire. Artist unknown. *Courtesy of the New-York Historical Society, New York City.*

Sir William Johnson has been well handled by James T. Flexner in his *Mohawk Baronet,* and William Smith has received a full treatment by L. F. S. Upton in his *The Loyal Whig.* Other than these, however, only Stanley Katz's *Newcastle's New York,* my own *Robert Livingston,* and Professor Bonomi's most recent *A Factious People* have emerged as major studies in the 15 years since those two essays issued a call for traditional history.

To turn more precisely to Professor Bonomi's approach, one warning must urgently be sounded. Many years ago—almost too many for comfort—Professor Judd and I served as research associates at Sleepy Hollow Restorations. In that capacity, we scurried through the archives of Westchester and New York counties, seeking additional light on the Philipse family. Both of us were astonished at the disreputable conditions in which we found those county archives. Fortunately, neither Professor Judd nor I suffered from acute asthma at that time. Dust, confusion, and disorder reigned; no organization, no sense of the documents' significance, and little aid for the scholar was available in either of the depositories. It seemed apparent that county archives retained their old records only because the law required them to do so, or because the archivists were too lethargic to dispose of them. Obviously, no one required that the collections be maintained with any semblance of propriety, or that they be made available for scholarly research. There are changes taking place, of course. The collections at Queens College in Flushing and at the State University in Stony Brook are refreshing, innovative breezes. Perhaps, as other scholars follow Professor Bonomi's lead, local archivists will treat the heritage in their possession with greater respect.

Such treatment is indeed necessary, because the history of New York, as Professor Klein so lucidly noted, is worthy of elaboration. His exposition of New York's diversity, which has also epitomized the development of the nation which surrounds it, touches upon a pregnant issue. He noted that "the more ethnically varied America became in the years that followed, the more attractive did Anglo-Saxon Jamestown and Plymouth appear to historians who themselves were disturbed by, and hostile to, the influx of masses of European immigrants." Perhaps the clearest expression of that hostility came, not too long ago, from the pen of Carl Bridenbaugh, then President of the American Historical Association:[3]

Today we must face the discouraging prospect that we all, teachers and pupils alike, have lost much of what this earlier generation possessed, the priceless asset of a shared culture. Today imaginations have become starved or stunted, and wit and humor, let alone laughter and a healthy frivolity, are seldom encountered. Furthermore, many of the younger practitioners of our craft, and those who are still apprentices, are products of lower middle-class or foreign origins, and their emotions not infrequently get in the way of historical reconstructions. They find themselves in a very real sense outsiders on our past and feel themselves shut out. This is certainly not their fault, but it is true. They have no experience to assist them, and the chasm between them and the Remote Past widens every hour. In our graduate schools we are training a host of skilled historical technicians, but all of us here, I think, will have to conclude that very few of our colleagues rise today to the high level of significant generalization or display either profound analytical powers or marked narrative proficiency. Certainly it is a great event when we get some living characterizations or credible vignettes of the actors of history, and it is an occasion for prolonged applause when we encounter any appreciation of beauty, taste, or humor. What I fear is that the changes observant in the background and training of the present generation will make it impossible for them to communicate to and reconstruct the past for future generations.

Despite such lamentations, the ranks of professional historians are becoming increasingly diversified, and in that diversification lies some hope for the history of the Middle Colonies. As those whose roots, either in practice or in longing, do not extend back to Anglican Jamestown, Puritan Boston, or Separatist Plymouth —as they become the scholars who examine our past, more and more of them may concern themselves with the polyglot Middle Colonies, and especially with the dynamic story of New York.

The history of New York, as Professor Klein has suggested, is the history of the United States. That New York's history has been neglected suggests perhaps that those who buy as well as those who write history prefer to deal with the illusion of what might have been rather than the reality of what we face. The more recent trend, particularly by so-called "radical" historians, to treat the "underside" of American history offers some hope that a more realistic appraisal of our past will be forthcoming. If so, if scholars are willing to treat the full panorama of our heritage, with its shame as well as its glory, then a rebirth of interest will occur in the history of the Middle Colonies and of colonial New York in particular.

Quantification and New York History

Irwin H. Polishook

THE ONSET of what social scientists call "quantification" has resulted in a new way of studying history. Defined rather narrowly, quantification may be understood simply as a synonym for counting, or the measurement and analysis of statistical material for the purpose of historical interpretation. More commonly, however, quantification refers to a method as well as to the content of judgments about the past. The availability of masses of information contained in such diverse sources as census reports, wills, tax lists, legislative records, and economic documents has long been known to historians and used at random to support their generalizations. But in utilizing this type of information, even when only a small selection of the whole evidence was sampled, the process of counting innumerable items was laborious and always imperfect. Today the method of counting is very different. Because of the availability of computers and highly refined mathematical programs, the entire body of almost any statistical series may be collected, collated, and compared. It is this special capacity, created by computer technology and computer-related sciences, that has made it possible for quantification to provide a new and unique dimension for the study of history.

The application of quantification to history is not unlimited. Certain problems, for example, do not lend themselves to study in this manner, because the questions they prompt are essentially qualitative in nature. Whether or not an American president was strong or weak, the causes of the American Revolution or the Civil War—these are precisely the kinds of subjects for which quantification can offer no satisfactory answers. Arthur Schlesin-

57

ger, Jr. probably put it too strongly, though not inaccurately, when he declared: "The *mystique* of empirical social research, in short, leads its acolytes to accept as significant only the questions to which the quantitative magic can provide answers. I am bound to reply that almost all important questions are important precisely because they are *not* susceptible to quantitative answers." Furthermore, for many periods of history not enough documentation remains for quantitative analysis. The loss of the greater part of the historical material makes it virtually impossible to do more than sample some of the evidence, methodologically not very different from the way in which historians have always studied the past.

At first consideration early American history might seem an unlikely field for the use of quantification. The absence of rich and reliable series of statistics limits severely the opportunities for quantification, while making the effort even more arduous. A number of historians, however, have forged ahead, despite the difficulties and occasionally disappointing results. Most notably, Jackson Turner Main has studied the legislative records of the Revolutionary states, counting every known vote and collecting all the remaining information about the men who sat in the state assemblies. The results have been illuminating, bearing substantially on the matter of whether these legislative bodies became more democratic because of the Revolution and on the nature of party divisions during the Confederation period. Likewise, by counting and comparing entire series of figures concerning marriages, births, and deaths in colonial Massachusetts Bay, historical demographers Philip Greven, John Demos, and Kenneth Lockridge have not only uncovered new information about the colonial family but have described how the family worked and analyzed its societal roles. Though the sources for quantitative studies of colonial America are relatively scarce, these scholars have shown the great potential residing in little-used and previously unworkable bodies of information.

The essays in this book by Thomas J. Archdeacon and Edwin G. Burrows depend on quantification for their basic methodology and conclusions. Both have dealt with subjects familiar to

Engraved by I. Carwithan, ca. 1730. Original in
the Bibliotheque Nationale, Paris.

colonial historians, but in both cases the sophisticated utilization of statistical documentation offers added insight into an old problem.

Archdeacon's paper, "The Age of Leisler: New York City, 1689–1710: A Social and Demographic Interpretation," focuses on the troubled period of New York City's history during and after Leisler's Rebellion, collecting all the available information about the city's inhabitants for the period under review. After analyzing and comparing with the aid of a new-generation computer, Archdeacon found that the tangled nature of New York politics associated with the name of Jacob Leisler since the late seventeenth century may best be understood within the context of ethnic differences and social conflict among the Dutch, English, and French population.

The Dutch of New York City rallied in support of Captain Jacob Leisler during the crisis in the province following the Glorious Revolution in England and the demise of the New England Confederation in America. Noting that the leaders and followers of Leisler's Rebellion were predominantly non-English, Archdeacon theorizes that the Leislerians were in some degree disgruntled and becoming misfits in a society undergoing rapid "Anglicanization." Moreover, Archdeacon shows that the political divisions of Leisler's Rebellion, which had arisen because of the displacement in power of the Dutch by the English, continued even after Jacob Leisler had been executed.

The essay by Burrows, "Military Experience and the Origins of the Federalism and Antifederalism," a paper on historical quantification, represents a different and somewhat older application of quantification, the collective biography, or as it is now called by some scholars, "prosopography." This is by no means a new undertaking for the historian. Several valuable works have concentrated on the analysis of elite groups in politics or business. Perhaps the most famous example for American history is Charles A. Beard's *An Economic Interpretation of the Constitution of the United States* (1913). Beard used the economic interests of the Founding Fathers as the basis of his conclusion that the personal wealth of the men who wrote the Constitution prompted the revision of the federal system. Of greater contemporary importance has been the work of Sir Lewis B. Namier, whose volumes on eighteenth-century England have revitalized our understanding of Great Britain and the North American colonies. Collective biography is now a respected and valid method of looking at history.

Using as his sample (or "universe," in the language of computer technology) a biographical profile of all 103 candidates to the New York State Ratifying Convention in 1787, Burrows found a significant correlation between the character of an individual's military service during the War for Independence and his position on the proposed Federal Constitution.

The thrust of Burrows' argument centers on the distinguishable pattern of Antifederalists who served in the state militia and Federalists whose military service took place in the Continental Army. He comments that militia service tended to reinforce a parochial attitude among men already state-oriented in their outlook. Militiamen, by and large, fought close to home, served with their neighbors, remained suspicious of units composed of strangers, and learned to rely for leadership on locally appointed officers. In contrast, members of the Continental Army fought under Congressionally appointed officers, served with men from the entire nation, and often were led to fight in regions far from home. Veterans of the Continental Army reacted vigorously to the weaknesses of the Articles of Confederation. They denounced the national government because it lacked the vital characteristics associated with their former military experience, namely, "energy, authority, discipline, reputation, [and] clarity of function."

Borrowing from the work of sociologist Robert K. Merton, Burrows suggests that the "fact" of military service helped to create for the militiamen a "localist political culture," while Continental service resulted in men of cosmopolitan attitude who had "a new sense of the requirements for national leadership."

Such articles as these demonstrate that much of the challenge implicit in early American history can be probed more effectively through the use of quantification. Archdeacon, for instance, by developing for the first time a demographic and social model of New York City's population, has been able to isolate the ethnic factor as a cause of Leisler's Rebellion and a continuing element in its prolonged aftermath. Oddly enough, though scholars have so often taken for granted the importance of ethnicity in the evolution of the Middle Colonies, the principal interpretations of Leisler's Rebellion (excepting Lawrence H. Leder's biographical study of Robert Livingston) have emphasized class conflict and sectionalism as the key variables in this dramatic event. Similarly, Burrows points to the failure on the part of historians to delve more systematically into the many factors that produce a political culture out of which men said either "yes" or "no" to the new federal system. Using the methods and materials of quantitative analysis, these authors have been able to throw light on underdeveloped aspects of our colonial past.

The Age of Leisler—New York City, 1689–1710: A Social and Demographic Interpretation

Thomas J. Archdeacon

I

COLONIAL HISTORIANS have traditionally neglected New York and have concentrated their research on Virginia and Massachusetts. The Old Dominion and the Bay Colony were the dominant provinces in their respective sections and were firebrands of the Revolutionary period. New York's history was lively but complicated, and few sources exist which clarify the issues. New Yorkers have aggravated the situation by permitting clerical inefficiency, bureaucratic myopia, governmental penuriousness, and accidental loss to destroy innumerable valuable records.

Implicit in the neglect of New York history is the unfortunate view that the colony, and especially its Manhattan Island port city, were atypical settlements. In the light of the general American experience neither Massachusetts nor Virginia was as relevant as New York. The first two were essentially homogeneous societies, and, indeed, the wealth of preserved records and the sense of heritage characteristic of these areas are a measure of their communal stability. The Bay Colony and the Old Dominion represent an ideal of unity cherished by Americans well aware of their diversity, while New York exemplifies the reality of pluralism alive with vigor and conflict. A tempestuous process of assimilation, recognizable even today, underlay the early years of the province and city of New York.

Governor Thomas Dongan in 1687 despairingly described the heterogeneity of New York. "Here bee not many of the Church

63

of England," he wrote; "few Roman Catholicks; abundance of
Quakers preachers men and Women especially; Singing Quakers;
Ranting Quakers, Sabbatarians; Antisabbatarians; Some Anabap-
tists some Independents; some Jews; in short of all sorts of opinions there are some and the most part of none at all."[1] Perhaps
New York was not so variegated as Dongan believed, but the
population did indeed have a mottled quality. As a pawn shut-
tled between the Netherlands and England, the province developed a polyglot image which its subsequent history as a
commercial entrepôt sustained.

Professors Evarts Boutwell Greene and Virginia Harrington
estimated that 2,732 people resided in New York City in 1703;[2]
and traces of these individuals have survived, scattered throughout the records of the municipality and the colony. Original tax
assessment rolls for July, September, and December, 1703, and
for February 1703–04,[3] and a copy, by the renowned editor
Edmund B. O'Callaghan, of a Manhattan census taken in
1703[4] mention the names of more than 1,000 persons dwelling in
the island's East, West, North, South, Dock, and Out Wards,
which then composed New York City. Omission of the rural Out
Ward and of citizens about whom almost nothing is known re-
duces this number to a group of 876 white individuals and heads
of families for whom partial or relatively complete biographical
data are available. Examination of this information by various
procedures including computer-aided statistical analysis reveals
much about New York City at the beginning of the eighteenth
century.

Four groups formed the basis of Manhattan's white population. Dutch settlers were the earliest European inhabitants of the
city and the most numerous contingent, including 374 identifiable New York families. The Dutch portion of the populace,
which was almost twice as large as the English segment, comprised 41 percent of the total of 876 and 56 percent of the 650
persons whose nationalities were discovered.[5]

English, French, and Jewish citizens made up the remainder
of the white residents. Few Englishmen immigrated to New
York before the capture of the city from the Dutch in 1664, and

To the Honourable

RIP VAN DAM. Esqr

PRESIDENT of His Majestys Council for the PROVINCE of NEW YORK

This View of the New Dutch Church is most humbly

Dedicated by your Honours most Obedient Servt Wm Burgis

The New Dutch Church in New York City, ca. 1731.
I. N. Phelps-Stokes, *Iconography of Manhattan Island*.

even after that date they gravitated to colonies where land was more available. Approximately 190 of the island's families were of Anglo-Saxon or Celtic stock; they accounted for 22 percent of the test sample and 29 percent of the ethnically identifiable group. Huguenots were the smallest numerically important white element. Seventy-four families had their roots in French soil; they constituted 8 percent of the test group and 11 percent of its ethnically recognizable portion. Only 12 of the 876 names belonged to Jews, but some among this handful were significant personalities in the community.

Occupational divisions in New York bore a strong relationship to the ethnic composition of the island's population. Englishmen and Frenchmen dominated the most important professions and were especially numerous among the merchant community; while Dutch residents, whose forebears had founded the city, pursued less prestigious activities. Although Dutch heads of families outnumbered their combined English and French counterparts by a margin of 110, only 36 Dutch but 61 English and French were merchants.

English birth or parentage was a major advantage for aspiring city merchants, because maintaining an extensive trade with the mother country was a prerequisite of great commercial success. Such activity demonstrated an ability to establish agency relationships and to obtain credit in England, and differentiated the mercantile elite from their less prosperous competitors. Huguenots and Jews duplicated these associations through colonies of coreligionists living in England and also fared well in commerce, but Dutch citizens were not so fortunate.

Assessment rolls, which represent the judgment of informed observers on the relative economic standing of every family within the city, suggest that the English and French who dominated the prestigious employments were the most well-to-do element of the population. In terms of both mean and median wealth English inhabitants formed the most prosperous ethnic group, while the descendants of the original Dutch settlers were financially second-class citizens. Distributing the members of each of the major national groups along a five-interval scale of

wealth[6] illustrates the nature of New York City's economic stratification in 1703 (Figure 1). The English seem strongest at the
highest end of the scale. The Dutch gravitate to the central
ranges and appear least frequently in the lowest and highest categories, a natural phenomenon under conditions of normal distribution. The French show concentrations in both the poorest and
richest brackets, a most peculiar arrangement which testifies to
the broad compass and thorough application of King Louis
XIV's program to discourage heresy.

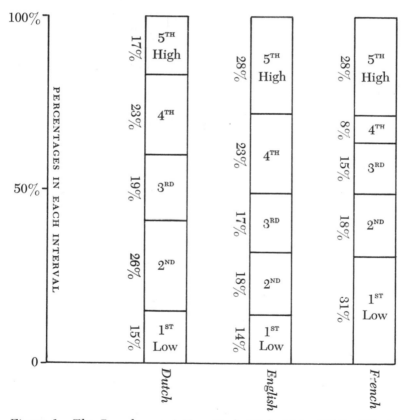

Figure 1—*The Prevalence of New York City's Major White Ethnic
Groups at Each Level of a Five-Interval Scale of Wealth Ascending
from the Poorest Group (Low) to the Most Affluent (High).*

Differences in economic standing were great in New York City, and a chasm sepaiated the elite from their fellow citizens. In terms of the tax lists, the most well-to-do 10 percent of the population controlled 47 percent of the community's wealth, and the top 20 percent possessed 69 percent of it. As for the approximate 20 percent of the populace who had assessments of only £5 they could not call even 3 percent of the total their own.

Assessment rolls only weakly reflect the great social change which must have been obvious to New Yorkers at the end of the seventeenth century. To the average Dutch citizen, whose family probably had resided in Manhattan for at least a generation, the upper classes must have seemed unduly foreign and filled with late English and French arrivals. The Dutch remained the most sizable group in every economic interval, but the burghers could not have found that fact comforting; the newer ethnic groups, in proportion to their numbers, bulked large among the wealthy. Indeed, the combined Anglo-French contingent outnumbered the Dutch in the highest interval (Figure 1).

Even residential patterns in Manhattan were symbolic and symptomatic of the late seventeenth-century transformation of New York from a Dutch to an English city. The Anglo-French group formed a majority of the inhabitants of the Dock Ward, which was located at the southeastern tip of the island and was the richest of the city's five central districts. In the North Ward, which was situated in the less desirable uptown area and was the poorest section, four of every five denizens were Dutch. Evidently, many descendants of New Amsterdam by 1700 found themselves relegated to the least attractive areas of the port town which their forebears had planted.

Changes such as occurred in New York City in the last third of the seventeenth century naturally produced tensions, but the structure of colonial society worked to prevent their translation into politics. Practicality demanded that monied men hold office, for they were the only persons with the financial means and the education requisite to execute the obligations effectively. Intellect and convention sanctified what necessity dictated and produced a characteristically deferential system. The candidates who came forward did not represent seriously divergent political or social positions, and, in many cases, elections were hardly contested.

Voting in the seventeenth and eighteenth centuries provided constitutional and symbolic affirmation to leaders who lacked substantive means of political coercion and who rested their authority on the legitimacy of their claim to govern. In New York the officeholding elite led the call for the right to elect local officials,[7] and evidently saw in the demand no threat to their security. Indeed, the leadership may have viewed the ballot as a means of guaranteeing their own position against the encroachment of higher authorities. In a system without parties and platforms, voters chose candidates with whom they strongly identified, and in any potential contests prominent natives would be likely to defeat the candidates of an outside agency.

In their quest for broadly based affirmation, the authorities tried to include as many people as possible in the political process. Approximately 224 of the 462 males 16 years of age or older in the East, West, and South Wards voted in the 1701 election. Undoubtedly some of the nonvoters were ineligible by virtue of being younger than the minimum age of 21, and so perhaps as much as 55 or 60 percent of the potential electorate cast a ballot. Of the 224 persons who participated, 38 (17 percent) ranked in the lowest bracket on the five-interval scale of wealth, a strong indication that economic restrictions on the exercise of the franchise were virtually nonexistent. Not even tenancy was a cause for disfranchisement. Only inhabitants who were underage or who did not reside in the district where they went to the polls had their ballots discarded.[8]

Voting was not designed to promote popular control of the government. Colonials theoretically did not hold political leaders responsible to their constituents, and considered factionalism neither desirable nor necessary. Disputed canvasses revealed cracks in the foundation of popular affirmation, and the contested elections in New York City in 1701 inspired the passage of legislation which sought to preserve "the peace, Welfare, and quiet of the Inhabitants Freeholders and Freemen" and to insure that "all heats Animosities Quarrels Strifes & Debates may for the future be laid aside & those already happened for ever hereafter be buried in Oblivion."[9]

The colonial political structure could silence the disaffected and maintain governmental stability until a crisis developed which destroyed the unity of the elite or tempted marginal leaders to challenge the more established. At that point voters gained an unintended opportunity to choose rather than to affirm, and elections allowed deep-rooted social divisions to become explosively evident. In New York City the Leislerian Rebellion and the ensuing years of bitterness provided such a set of circumstances.

II

Jacob Leisler and his followers were the products of the societal dislocation caused by the transformation of New York into an English city. Indeed, the inability of the Leislerians and the Anti-Leislerians to identify themselves except by reference to the protagonist suggests that they had difficulty in defining their differences. Despite mutual accusations of hypocrisy, both groups shared an allegiance to the Glorious Revolution and the Protestant religion and did not disagree seriously in political philosophy.

Leisler migrated to New Amsterdam in 1660 as a twenty-year-old soldier in the employ of the Dutch West India Company. Born in Frankfurt-am-Main, he was the son of a Calvinist pastor, and probably grew up in a more substantial situation than his modest status upon arrival implied. Leisler's marriage in 1663 to Elsje Tymens, the widow of the wealthy merchant Pieter Cornelisen Van der Veen, provided him with capital to trade in furs, tobacco, and wines; and he soon gained a place among the community's most affluent members. The union also made him an in-law of the foremost families of the province, including the Loockermans, Bayards, and Van Cortlandts.[10]

Despite a contentious personality, Leisler played a continuing role in public affairs. He served as a mediator in the legal system of New Amsterdam and was a Deacon of the Reformed Church. During the Dutch reoccupation of 1673 to 1674, Leisler was close to Governor Anthony Colve, who placed him on a five-man commission to assess the estates of Manhattan's most affluent citizens for tax purposes. His relationship with the English authorities was not as strong; and, although he remained locally prominent as a captain of militia, he had reached the periphery and not the center of the colonial power structure.[11]

In the 1680's Leisler's position of influence declined when Charles II and James II took action to expand the royal prerogative by establishing the Dominion of New England of which Massachusetts was the head and New York the heart. Although the Bay Colony's leadership complained that a coterie of eight New Yorkers on the royally appointed 42-man Council exerted undue political influence on Governor Edmund Andros, not all Hudson River politicians were intimates of the executive; and only the elite helped guide the fortunes of the combined provinces. Local leaders suffered a relative loss of position as New York became an outpost of Massachusetts, an outcome which led Leisler later to write disparagingly about the narrow distribution of power under the reorganized government.[12]

In New England, after the Glorious Revolution, the indigenous leadership united to overthrow the Dominion government. In New York, after William of Orange's landing at Torbay, the most important residents remained loyal to the regime which they dominated; and men of less renown came forward to challenge their right to rule. The ensuing struggle for power fed upon the ethnic and social divisions within the population, and died out only as time transformed the composition of the community.

Jacob Leisler, so long on the periphery of power, emerged as the leader of the New York uprising. The circumstances suited perfectly his thwarted ambitions, his antipathy for the ruling clique with whom he had feuded, and his exaggerated religious sensitivities. Characteristically and with probable sincerity he associated his personal enemies "who under the appearance of the functions of the Protestant religion, remain still affected to the Papist" with a grand evil plot to stymie the wills of God and king.[13]

Various considerations, including the allegiance of family relationships, motivated Leisler's aides. Jacob Milborne, who became Leisler's chief aide, returned from a voyage to Europe in August, 1689 and joined the rebellion; a widower, he married the captain's daughter Mary in the following year. Milborne, whose Baptist beliefs differed from those of New York's Anglican establishment, had occasionally clashed with the provincial government, and had once successfully sued Andros in an English court for false arrest. Robert Walters, the insurgents' alderman from the South Ward, was the husband of another Leisler daughter, Catharina, whom he married in 1685. Samuel Edsall, Milborne's former father-in-law, served as Queens County's representative to Leisler's Council, and his connection with the rebel commander may have gained his three sons-in-law, Benjamin Blagge, Pieter De La Noy, and William Lawrence, their seats on that body.[14]

Some Leislerian leaders were English, but the movement bore an unmistakable Dutch aura. Judging by those who stood trial with Captain Leisler in 1691, his closest associates, except for Milborne and Edsall, were all Dutch. Usually survivors or descendants of New Amsterdam, these men found it difficult or impossible to adjust to the new social order created by the "Anglicization" of the city.

Pieter De La Noy, New York's only elected mayor prior to the nineteenth century and a member of Leisler's Council, emigrated from Haarlem in the Netherlands, and in 1680 married Elizabeth De Potter, the widow of Isaac Bedlow, a member of an old New Amsterdam family. De La Noy later married a daughter of Samuel Edsall. Abraham Gouverneur, the town clerk during the revolt, was born in 1671, the son of Nicholas Gouverneur, a prominent Netherlands merchant who had traded with New Amsterdam. The young man's mother, Machteldt De Reimer Gouverneur, was the daughter of an established Dutch Manhattan family and remained a resident of the island after the English conquest. The physician Samuel Staats, who served on Leisler's Council, was the classic example of a New Netherlander drawn to the rebellion. The son of Major Abraham Staats, Samuel left the colony when the English arrived in 1664 and returned only after the Prince of Orange landed at Torbay.[15]

Nicholas Bayard, the chief antagonist of Leisler and his followers during and after the uprising, persistently claimed that the insurgents were merely a "parcel of ignorant and innocent people, almost none but of the Dutch nation." Leisler won their support, according to Bayard, with assurances that William would end English administrative control of New York and would govern New York as his own Dutch fief. Bayard's hatred of the rebel leader doubtlessly distorted his outlook, but he did have an insight into the nature of the conflict. Leisler was sensitive to these charges and tried to deny them, but all indicators, including even the sharp decline in participation at the Reformed Church following the pastor's denunciation of the captain, point to deep Dutch involvement.[16]

New York's rebellion was not a conspiracy to restore Dutch rule, but rather a spontaneous outpouring of resentment by a segment of the population which, if the patterns of 1700 held true a decade earlier, found itself dispossessed of the city founded by its fathers. When the Dominion collapsed in 1689, two groups vied for the population's affirmation of its claim to control of New York City. Lieutenant Governor Francis Nicholson, Anthony Brockholst, Nicholas Bayard, Stephen Van Cortlandt, and their associates represented the English ruling clique and the Dutch elite who enjoyed success within the new order. Leisler and his followers appealed to those longing for older, better days. With the elite seriously divided, colonial New Yorkers had a rare opportunity to choose their leaders rather than merely to ratify their right to office.

Despite Leisler's pretensions to provincial domain as "lieutenant governor," the uprising remained a peculiarly New York City affair, and attracted little support in areas where the English conquest had not seriously altered the social structure. Milborne was unable to persuade the Albanians to abandon their old

elite, and Leisler did not maintain sustained communication with
the anti-Dominion insurgents on Long Island, who looked more
to Boston than to Manhattan for direction. Although Leisler appointed Councillors from Orange and Westchester Counties,
neither of these areas seems to have contributed substantially to
the rebellion.[17]

England's Glorious Revolution and the accession of the Prince
of Orange to the throne inspired Dutch New Yorkers and gave
these second-class citizens a psychological thrust to reassert
themselves. Their expression took a form analogous to the pre-in-
dustrial urban phenomenon described by Eric Hobsbawm and
George Rudé as the "church and king riot," a dual uprising by
the common people in the defense of unassailable conservative
institutions but against the upper classes traditionally associated
with them.[18] In Leisler's Rebellion Dutch Calvinist New Yorkers
overthrew their English Anglican government in the name of the
English crown and its Episcopal religion, a paradox made pa-
thetically rational by their affectionate identification with the
new monarch.

"Papist" was Leisler's favorite epithet, but few of his avowed
enemies resided in New York at the time. Curiously, but true to
the "church and king" pattern, the Leislerians directed their
wrath at their English Protestant neighbors, who were logically
their allies. The rich merchants and affluent tradesmen of the
group earned special scorn. Bands of rebels beat John Crooke
and Edward Taylor, and Leisler from time to time arrested or
seized the goods of Robert Allison, Thomas Clark, Philip French,
William Merritt, John Merritt, and William Nicolls. The insurgents even left the confines of New York City to break into the
house of Daniel Whitehead, a Queens County Justice of the
peace.[19]

Frenchmen and renegade Dutch burghers who associated
closely with the English or held positions of trust within the government also received harsh treatment. Leisler's men allegedly
commandeered seven full and six half barrels of gunpowder be-
longing to Gabriel Minvielle, a native of Bordeaux who acted as
mayor in the 1684–85 term.[20] Leisler arrested Jacob De Key and

Brandt Schuyler, both representatives of wealthy Dutch families, and Derrick Vanderburgh, a Dutch mason who later became a member of Trinity Church, the Anglican house of worship.[21] The rebel chieftain treated the vitriolic Nicholas Bayard with understandable hostility and kept him in prison for several months.[22]

Jacob Leisler almost undid the social fabric of New York City, and the decision of his enemies to execute him after his downfall in 1691 was a measure of their fright. His rebellion had its roots in the individual and group frustrations which developed from the changes wrought by 25 years of English rule. Unfortunately, Leisler's successes did not retrieve the happy past which history had stolen, and his ultimate failure bequeathed only intensified antagonisms to the future.

Governor Henry Sloughter and his successor Benjamin Fletcher were unsympathetic with the rebel faction in New York. During Fletcher's tenure the Anti-Leislerians seized the spoils of victory, and the governor became infamous for his huge land grants to his allies. Symbolically the passage of the Ministry Act of 1693, under which the authorities gave stipends to an Anglican clergyman, and the erection of Trinity Church were the high points of these years. By 1695 political vagaries brought the Whigs to power in England; and two years later the new administration dismissed the Tory Fletcher and appointed an Irish peer, Richard Coote, the Earl of Bellomont, in his stead.

Bellomont, an opponent of Fletcher in England, naturally found his allies in New York among the Leislerians. He quickly recognized the role of ethnicity in dividing the city's people and condemned the clique which surrounded his predecessor for aggravating the situation by attempting to appropriate the sobriquet of "English party." The new governor complained that Fletcher had "supported a few rascally English who are a scandall to their nation and the Protestant Religion . . . and severely used the Dutch, except some few Merchants, whose trade he favored, who ought to have an equal benefit of the English Governt who are most hearty for his present Majty and are a sober industrious people and obedient to Governt."[23]

Enemies of the Earl denounced him for filling the Assembly

and the militia with mean, indigent Dutch; and William Vesey, Trinity's pastor, protested to Archbishop Tenison in England that "our Governor has used all methods to destroy us and support dissenters." Nicholas Bayard, writing shortly after Bellomont's death on March 5, 1701, succinctly expressed the feelings of the Anti-Leislerian faction: "Till the day of his death most of the meanest and those of Dutch extractions have been put in all the offices and places of trust and power; by which means most of the principal and peaceable inhabitants and especially those of the English nation have been opprest."24

Lieutenant Governor John Nanfan, Bellomont's nephew, became the Chief Crown officer in New York upon his uncle's death. During Nanfan's tenure as interim executive the Leislerians and the Anti-Leislerians fought bitterly for the control of the city and colony. On the municipal level, the struggle culminated in Manhattan's disputed elections of 1701, which again laid bare the bases of social and political divisions within the city.

III

Both Leislerian and Anti-Leislerian candidates claimed victory in the elections for Alderman and Assistant in the East, West, and South Wards, and each group demanded that the new mayor, Thomas Noell, recognize its claims. Upon taking office on October 14, 1701, Noell appointed three quartets of investigators, including two members of each faction on every board, to examine the returns in the disputed districts. The Leislerians, believing that Noell, an Englishman, would not be impartial or fearing that their successes would not bear scrutiny, refused to participate. In all three contested wards, the Anti-Leislerian poll checkers declared their candidates to be the victors, but evidently a compromise provided the final solution. The Leislerians took the seats in the East Ward, and the Anti-Leislerians assumed the posts in the West and South Wards. The original Anti-Leislerian winners in the Dock Ward and the Leislerian victors in the North Ward retained their seats.25

As part of the election procedure, officials in the wards recorded the names of all the persons who cast ballots for each candidate. During the investigation the examiners reviewed these polls and the Common Council published them as evidence in their *Minutes*.[26] These returns provide not only information about the divisions within the city's leadership, but are also an untapped source of materials on the bases of popular support enjoyed by each faction. Approximately 224 of the 738 males in the sample population used in this survey appear on the lists; and full data on ethnic background, economic standing, commercial activity, and occupational pursuit are available for 213 of them.

Examination of the election returns indicates that in the years after Leisler's death the struggle between his supporters and opponents retained its essentially ethnic quality. Statistical analysis using multiple regression tests on a General Electric 635 computer shows that national background was by far the most important factor in distinguishing the Leislerian and the Anti-Leislerian rank-and-file. The ethnic variable was highly related to voting behavior in a manner which rules out coincidental occur-

TABLE I

Factors Affecting Political Party Affiliation
in the New York City Elections of 1701 *

Total Variation Explained: 56%

Variables	Part. Corr. Coef.	T-Value	Prop. Cum. Var., in %
Ethnic background	−0.69542	−13.78812	53.8
Date of marriage	0.00442	0.06300	00.0
Employment and social positions			
Skilled and unskilled trades	0.19843	2.88453	00.6
Services	0.13279	1.91144	00.0
Food production and distribution	0.15558	2.44030	00.1
Seafaring trades	0.18511	2.68384	00.3
Merchants and gentlemen	0.16898	2.44279	01.3
Economic standing	0.04798	0.68447	00.0
Relative mercantile importance	−0.11793	−1.69211	00.6

*Results of BMD 03R Multiple Regression Program Testing

rence in 999 cases out of 1,000. With all the other factors held constant, ethnicity independently accounted for an extraordinarily high 54 percent of the variation in voting behavior (Table I).

Dutch residents gave overwhelming loyalty to the Leislerian candidates; 133 of the 224 voting males were recognizable Hollanders, and 111 of them (83 percent) cast their ballots for Leislerian office-seekers. The Leislerians won without dispute in the North Ward, where the Dutch comprised 78 percent of the population, and lost decisively in the Dock Ward, the only district where the English and French formed a majority. Englishmen and Frenchmen were almost unanimously Anti-Leislerian, with 59 out of 68 (87 percent) of the former and 40 out of 41 (98 percent) of the latter choosing candidates from that faction.

Wealth did not significantly affect political affiliation. In terms of the five-interval scale of economic standing, the two factions were almost equally represented in every category, save for an unusually large number of Anti-Leislerians in the lowest range (Figure 2). Nor did occupational background strongly affect political preferences. Only ten merchant voters supported Leislerian candidates, while 30 cast their ballots for the opposition; but even in this instance the breakdown followed ethnic more than professional lines. Of the 10 Leislerian merchants, 8 were Dutch; and of the 29 Anti-Leislerian traders whose nationalities were known, 24 were English or French. The political affiliations of the cordwainers similarly suggest the ethnic basis of New York's political divisions. Of the 16 cordwainers who cast ballots, 15 were Leislerians and only one was an Anti-Leislerian, but all of the former were Dutch and only the latter was an Englishman.

Age bore a subtle relation to political preference. Judging from data obtained about 107 of the voters, Leislerian candidates drew their strongest support from Dutch New Yorkers who married between 1686 and 1695. Born around the time of the English conquest, these persons represented the first generation to feel its full impact on the province's social structure. Aliens in their homeland, they found Leisler's movement an especially attractive opportunity and call to assert themselves; in 1701, out of

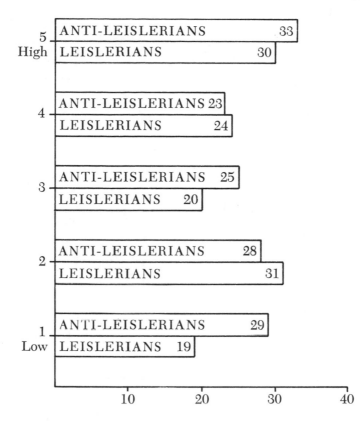

Figure 2—*Distribution of Voters with Identified Ethnic Backgrounds on a Five-Interval Scale of Wealth Ascending from the Poorest Group (Low) to the Most Affluent (High).*

24 of them, 23 (98 percent) voted for Leislerian candidates. Leislerism exerted a powerful but more modest influence on the oldest and youngest members of the Dutch community. Of the 20 who took spouses between 1676 and 1685, 15 (75 percent) cast their ballots for the faction's candidates in 1701, while 25 (76 percent) of the 33 wed after 1695 did the same (Figure 3).

Englishmen and Huguenots, regardless of age, uniformly opposed the Leislerians. Neither group could find any relevance in a movement of displaced Dutchmen, and the English were able

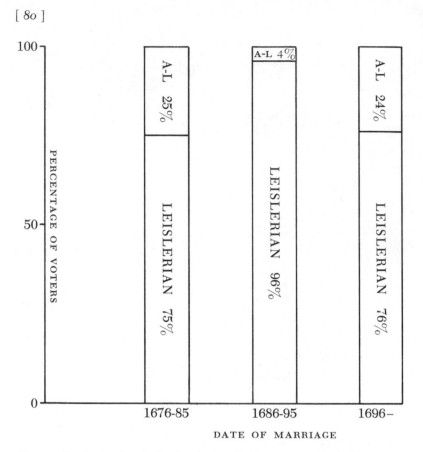

Figure 3—*Strength of the Leislerian Party among Dutch Voters in Various Age Groups.*

to identify with their countrymen among the Anti-Leislerian leadership. Of the 40 voters in the Anglo-French community for whom marriage dates are available, 35 (88 percent) cast their ballots for Anti-Leislerians.

Spawned as a protest against the "Anglicization" of New York City, the Leislerian agitation grew weaker as the transformation neared completion. The growing numerical strength of the English and the French and the passing away of burghers who remembered or learned from their parents of the halcyon days of Dutch rule brought an end to the first chapter in the history of ethnic conflict in New York City. The composite voter-marriage

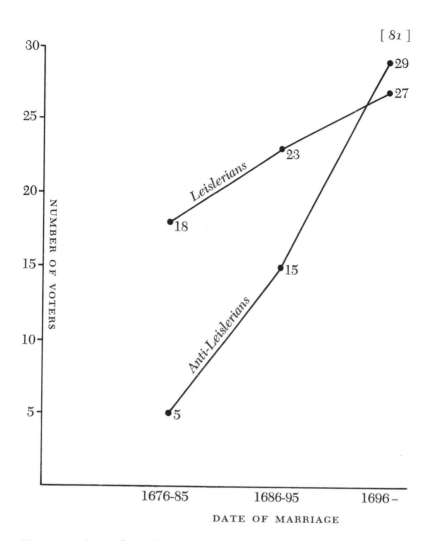

Figure 4—*Strength of the Leislerians and the Anti-Leislerians among New York City Voters of Various Age Groups.*

date statistics in Figure 4 succinctly delineate the history of the period. The Leislerians captured 78 percent of the voters who wed between 1676 and 1685 and 61 percent of those who took spouses between 1686 and 1695. When Englishmen and Frenchmen began to appear among the youngest voters, as represented by those who assumed family responsibilities after 1696, their ballots permanently shifted the majority to the Anti-Leislerians.

IV

New York City's colonial experience suggests some points of general interest for the study of early America. Historians must include all strata of society in their investigations, because the relationships among these elements determined much of each community's development. Researchers can gather adequate demographic sources for the examination of even large urban areas and can statistically analyze the data quickly and accurately through the application of various mechanical processing techniques.

In seeking the dynamics of conflicts in the colonial period, scholars should also give greater emphasis to more abstract "cultural" factors. At least until the time of the American Revolution, the leadership of the provinces came from a social and economic elite which shared a common political philosophy and which did not attempt to appeal to the "class interests" of the masses of the electorate. In such a situation, the voters chose candidates with whom they identified on the basis of characteristics such as ethnic background or religion.

Finally, the New York City experience indicates that historians should attempt to define more precisely the concept of an American nationality and reconsider its validity as a unifying theme for the colonial period. Learning to live in a society composed of diverse elements was a great problem for the men of the seventeenth and eighteenth centuries, who had often fled Europe to avoid the penalties of life in a heterogeneous environment. Examination of the process by which they came to tolerate each other and to recognize themselves as members of a single continental community remains a vital project for the discipline and a challenge for its scholars.

Military Experience and the Origins of Federalism and Antifederalism

Edwin G. Burrows

I

For at least several generations now historians have been trying to decide whether the dispute between Federalists and Antifederalists over the federal Constitution touched broader conflicts within the social and political structures of post-Revolutionary America; and if so, what kind—conflicts between classes, interest groups, geographic sections, legislative factions, or perhaps something entirely different? This lively and important controversy has special significance among the proponents of what is these days called "quantification"; for, beginning with the work of Orin G. Libby and Charles A. Beard, it has generated a unique literature of attempts to resolve a historical problem through the systematic compilation and analysis of measureable data.[1]

At the same time this literature offers some comfort to those who find quantification objectionable, for as one surveys its results the suspicion arises that quantification here, if not elsewhere, has yielded remarkably few fresh insights into the problem despite all the tables and calculations it has produced. One might fairly wonder, indeed, if quantification is not becoming an end in itself, more and more concerned with gathering statistics than exploring what the statistics mean. The aim of the present essay, however, is to explore what some of the statistics may mean, and in so doing to suggest a new conceptual framework within which quantification may yet lead to a better understanding of what divided Federalists and Antifederalists.

83

Let us begin by examining the military backgrounds of the 54 Antifederalists and 49 Federalists who are known to have stood for election to the New York ratifying convention, which met in Poughkeepsie during June and July of 1788.[3] Not surprisingly, two-thirds of the 103 candidates had carried arms against the British in the Revolutionary War, most as commissioned officers at the regimental level or above. What is unexpected, however, is the pronounced correlation between Antifederalism and militia experience on the one hand and, on the other, between Federalism and service in the Continental Army. Of 26 Continental veterans, 18 were Federalists; of 42 militia veterans, 32 were Antifederalists. Four of every five Antifederalist veterans had served in the state militia, while two of every three Federalist veterans had served in the Continentals.[4] On careful inspection this emerges as one of the sharpest differences between the collective career-profiles of the two groups, and it cannot be explained away as a function of, say, occupation or place of residence.[5] More intriguing still, military experience as such was rarely if ever mentioned in contemporary sources as a way to distinguish between opponents and supporters of the Constitution, nor does it figure prominently in historical accounts of the ratification contest. Quantification without interpretation is always futile; in this case, clearly enough, our data compel us to find a fresh approach to the old question of what kinds of people became Federalists and Antifederalists.

As a first step, consider Robert K. Merton's famous distinction between "cosmopolitan" and "local" influentials.[6] While studying interpersonal influence in "Rovere," a small town on the eastern seaboard, Merton encountered these two types of influentials living side by side. He called them "cosmopolitans" and "locals" because the chief distinction between them was their orientation toward the community. The local influential concentrated his attention on local affairs, gauging the significance of even major international events by their immediate implications for the life of the town, and expressing deep attachment to those local habits and conventions which he believed set Rovere apart from all other communities. The cosmopolitan influential, though he en-

The following Gentlemen appointed Captains, by the Provincial Congrefs, for the inliftment of volunteers, to enter into fervice, for the defence of the Liberties of America, in the firft Battallion to be raifed in the City of New-Ycrk, under the command of the Colonels M Dougal, and Ritzema, have thought proper to make public, the following places of rendezvous, and the encouragement to volunteers

CAPTAIN John Weiffenvelt, and Capt. Gerfhom Mott, at Mr. Fofter Lewis's, innholder, near Beekman's flip. Captain Willet, at Mr. Abraham Van Dyck's, innholder in the Broadway. Captain Jacob Cheefman, at Mr. John Rutter's, in Cherry ftreet. Capt. Samuel Broome, at Mr. Fofter Lewis's. Capt John Quackenbos, at Mr. Abraham Van Dyck's, Mr. Edward Bardin's Chapel ftreet, innholder, and Mr. Fofter Lewis's. Capt. John Johnfon, at Mr. Edward Bardin's. Capt. William Goforth, at Mr. Abraham Van Dyck's. Captain Lieutenant John Copp, acting in the abfence of Capt. Richard Vaarick, private Seéretary to General Schuyler, at Capt. Jofiah Banks, in Little Dock ftreet, near the Exchange, and at Mr William Mariner's, in Horfe and Cart ftreet, innholders. Capt. Van Wyck, at Mr. Abraham Van Dyck's.

Volunteers, from the time of their inliftment, to enter into immediate pay, at one fhilling and eleven pence per day ; and alfo to receive one dollar per week, until they are encamped. in order to enable them to fupport themfelves in the intermediate time ; and they are likewife to be provided with a fuit of regimental clothes, a firelock, ammunition, accoutrements, and every other article neceffary for the equipment of AMERICAN SOLDIERS.

GOD fave the CONGRESSES

Announcement of the raising of a battalion of Continental soldiers in New York as it appeared in *The New-York Journal; or, The General Advertiser*, July 27, 1775. *Courtesy of The New-York Historical Society, New York City.*

joyed little or no influence beyond the community proper, was far more attentive to matters outside it. He saw himself as a functioning part of a larger society, and he demonstrated hardly any of the sentimental affection for mere neighborhood so characteristic of his localist counterparts.

Antecedent to these contrasting orientations, Merton went on to say, were basic differences in the career patterns of local and cosmopolitan influentials. Local influentials had been born and educated and always employed in Rovere itself; Rovere people were the only people they knew well, and the only people who knew them well. Getting ahead and acquiring influence there had meant the formation of an elaborate web of close personal contacts and the slow accumulation of insights into the social, economic, and political life of the community. Cosmopolitan influentials, by contrast, had made their marks in business or the professions outside Rovere and could claim none of the locals' almost intuitive understanding of or sympathy for the people and affairs of the town. Instead, their influence derived from the possession of worldly expertise, information, and interests not to be found among home-grown influentials: how many people they knew in the community mattered less than what they knew.

For our purposes, Merton's distinction between cosmopolitan and local influentials in Rovere has double value. It alerts us, for one thing, to the exceedingly complex interrelations of social experience and life-style with fundamental political orientation: in twentieth-century Rovere or eighteenth-century New York, the ways men think about public matters and the ways they live and work overlap at innumerable points. Once again, no mere statement of those points in statistical form can suffice to describe their human texture and meaning. More important, however, Merton's study of Rovere can provide us with a conceptual framework for assessing the contribution of divergent military experiences to the ratification controversy. The distinction between cosmopolitan and local influentials, with all it implies about contrasting orientations and career-patterns, instructs us that we need not locate some basic social or economic antagonism between veterans of the militia and veterans of the Continental Line in New York to support the hypothesis that, on this ground alone, they would have had much to disagree about— that service in those two organizations gave rise to sharply conflicting attitudes and impressions about American politics and society, attitudes and impressions that would meet head on a half-dozen years after the fighting had ended. Our next step, then, is to consider what we can learn about the nature of the militia and Continental experiences that would tend to sustain such an hypothesis.

II

The militia, for its part, demanded and maintained loyalties during the Revolutionary War that would conflict with the growth of new, national allegiances. However inefficient or unreliable it might have been against British regulars, the militia was one of those primary institutions of community life that survived the Revolutionary upheaval without notable changes in design or purpose. The state Assembly never tampered with its two most cherished and basic traditions: a conscription of all able-bodied males in the community, and a strict decentralization of responsibility for enlistments, training, discipline, and, on occasion, tactics as well.[7] Almost inevitably, these structural continuities would have operated to filter and deflect currents of nationalist feeling stirred by intercolonial cooperation during the war.

But function, in all likelihood, mattered much more than structure, for the militia also narrowed the range of possible contributions to the war effort while intensely localizing their costs. We do the militiaman no disservice to note that it was the rare militia company or battalion that got a chance to strike a telling blow for national independence. Likely as not, an engagement with the enemy promised little more than an indecisive skirmish followed by a grim accounting of trampled crops, slaughtered livestock, burned-out homesteads, and casualties among friends and relatives. Every family in the upper Mohawk Valley, for example, reportedly lost at least one man at Oriskany; and, at war's end, Montgomery County alone, having fewer than 3,500 males between 16 and 60, put its costs at 150,000 bushels of wheat,

700 destroyed buildings, 1,200 abandoned farms, 380 widows, and 2,000 fatherless children.[8] Obliged to take his stand on home ground, to reckon the success or failure of his efforts in social as well as military terms, the militiaman would be poorly prepared, from this perspective at least, to believe that the final British capitulation proved anything but his own ability to endure schemes of oppression hatched in the world beyond his own community. The idea that the Constitution was a fulfillment of a common Revolutionary struggle on the field of battle—an idea often put forth by Federalists in the ratification debates—was by no means immediately obvious in light of the militiaman's own experiences.[9]

Closely related to all this is the probability that militia service helped to reinforce and perpetuate traditional impressions of an insurmountable cultural diversity among the American people. No one, of course, could be absolutely certain that 4,000,000 people scattered over 900,000 square miles of wilderness had enough in common to coexist peacefully. But Antifederalists insisted that the heterogeneity of the Americans was a major objection to ratifying the new Constitution—no national government, they said, could superintend such a population; if it did, it was not likely to remain republican. Here, unmistakably, an accent of empirical certainty intrudes upon received republican theory, the certainty of men who had passed through a great anticolonial revolution without learning whether their countrymen were in fact so intolerably different as they seemed at a distance.[10] By localizing the energies and emotions of war, in short, the militia served to accentuate parochial feelings at a time when other forces were working to break them down.

Finally, the militia experience had much to do with the formation of a distinctively localist political culture. On the muster ground or battlefield, the militia brought together the electorate of the district and county and gave them a chance to sort out those among them most worthy of confidence and respect. To hold a command at the company or regimental level, as many Antifederalist candidates for the New York ratifying convention had done, suggests a high degree of personal rapport with

the local citizen-soldiers, a rapport that could be turned to politi-
al advantage when the community later sought men to represent it in the councils of government. Few New York Antifederalist leaders enjoyed the influence of family, wealth, education,
or connections, though by 1788 virtually all had nonetheless
found their way through a maze of local offices into county
courts or the state legislature. It was the militia, one strongly
suspects, that first boosted many of these able and ambitious,
but otherwise undistinguished, men out of obscurity and into the
public arena. But still more important, it was in the militia that
the value of personal, face-to-face relations between the represented and their representatives became a vital element in the
day-to-day political assumptions and expectations of the men
who would resist ratification of the Constitution. Their very ca-
reers depended on such relations, yet the Constitution, by pro-
posing the creation of extensive electoral districts and low ratios
of representation, promised to establish a political system in
which all the advantages would lie with those who could appeal, say, to superior rank or education rather than to an inti-
mate knowledge of community life.[11]

For those candidates to the New York convention who had
served in the Continental Army, however, everything was different. To begin with, the Army itself, though a deliberate imitation
of existing British models and commanded by men whose military thinking was decidedly orthodox, was nonetheless one of
the genuinely revolutionary innovations of the Revolution.[12]
Created by a Continental Congress still speaking in the name of
an entity called the "Twelve Confederated Colonies," it was, in
theory, a national institution that antedated the formal appearance of the nation—a symbol of colonial desires for coordinated
action and the first instrument of an effectively continental policy. On the battlefield, it was meant to be what the militia was
not—aggressive, mobile, and professional. Off the battlefield, as
an organization unencumbered in theory by traditional loyalties,
it took unprecedented steps toward a rational exploitation of the
nation's human and material resources. The Army's performance,
it need hardly be added, ordinarily fell short of expectations, but

even blundering its way to victory the institution itself stimulated and attracted new social values and interstate loyalties.[13]

The experience of campaigning with the Army from New England to the Carolinas in the company of Virginians and Rhode Islanders developed those new interstate loyalties still further. Parochial attachments and assumptions of an overwhelming cultural diversity in the country became more and more difficult to support, and what gradually took their place was the conviction that the war not only freed the colonies but created a nation.[14] Then, too, if service in the Army and loyalty to it as a national institution accustomed some men to thinking in continental generalities, it also bred an early discontent with the Articles of Confederation, which appeared to have institutionalized the very values and sentiments the Army was meant to overcome.

That the Confederation had, to all intents and purposes, outlasted the Army was a cruel twist of fate indeed for those who had briefly experienced the thrill of continental solidarity; and what Richard B. Morris has described as the Founding Fathers' postwar nightmare of "drift toward anarchy culminating in a crisis" easily and not surprisingly often took on the flavor of a military reversal in Federalist rhetoric.[15] More to the point, it was not at all accidental that in their campaign to supplant the Articles of Confederation, Federalists would accent those virtues of national government—energy, authority, discipline, reputation, clarity of function, specificity of purpose—the absence of which would particularly frustrate the veteran of Continental service. It was as though the ideally efficient national system had, in some subtle fusion of experience and ideology, taken on the same properties as an ideally efficient national army.

The veteran of Continental service would also be likely to appreciate that certain institutions were especially guilty of promoting local attachments at the expense of more generous national sentiments. Not least among these institutions, of course, was the militia itself, which had long excited the contempt of professional soldiers for its failure to respond to the same imperatives and values as the regular Army.[16] What the Continentals saw as the militia's insensitivity to the national interest gave them an object-lesson in the connection between social orientation and institutional structure, only one result of which was an erosion of traditional antipathies toward standing armies in the employ of central authorities. The conceit that a militia system could suffice as the bulwark of the nation, Hamilton noted sourly in *The Federalist*, No. 25, "had like to have lost us our independence." No less than a dozen more of the essays that he, Jay, and Madison produced for the Federalist cause in New York were devoted, wholly or in part, to the proposition that the vitality as well as the safety of a truly national government would depend on its power to raise and support a military establishment distinct from the militia.[17]

Finally, if it is correct that the militia experience contributed to the formation of a localist political culture, then it is in the experience of Continental service that we can locate some roots of an alternative, cosmopolitan political culture. The Army, from this angle of vision, had helped create a new sense of the requirements for national leadership. Expertise, a knowledge of men and events around the country, an ability to transcend parochial attachments, and a feeling for distinctly national goals, not to say a belief in an American nationality itself—all of these would emerge in the Army as correctives to the community-oriented, affective political values essential for a public career in the militiaman's world.

The rub was, however, that under the Articles of Confederation cosmopolitanism carried little weight and may indeed have been something of a disability. One finds, for example, that fewer and fewer New York Federalists had been able (or cared) to win elective office in the years after Independence. Eleven Federalist and 14 Antifederalist candidates had attended the fourth provincial congress of 1777, which drew up the first state constitution; but a mere five Federalists had sat in the most recent session of the Assembly before the Poughkeepsie convention, amid a phalanx of 18 Antifederalists. The peculiar genius of the Constitution lay in its promise to create a new arena of effective activity for men whose ability to visualize and work for distinctly national interests—an ability owing more than a little to

their service in the Continental Army—could not be utilized
under the Confederation system.[18]

III

Military experience was, of course, only a single element in the
personal histories of the Poughkeepsie candidates. Its contribution to their disagreement over the proposed federal Constitution
cannot be isolated from the effects of socioeconomic status, kin-
ship and associational relations, geographic mobility, political experience, ethnic and religious identification, and the like. The
appropriate conclusion to these brief impressions and specula-
tions, then, is not that the ratification controversy should be understood as a conflict between veterans of the state militia and
veterans of the Continental Line among the convention
candidates.[19] It is, rather, that their divergent military backgrounds strongly suggest that the leading Federalists and Antifederalists in New York were very different sorts of people—different not necessarily in the possession of competing social or economic interests, but different, like Merton's cosmopolitan and
local influentials, because the kinds of lives they led disposed
them to conflicting assumptions about the nature of their common country and the changes likely to be forced upon it by
adopting a more centralized form of national government. Here
we return to the issue with which we began, for we cannot pursue this promising suggestion further without the precise, systematically analyzed knowledge of their private and public ca-
reers that quantification alone can provide. However moribund
or fruitless it has been of late, quantification may yet deepen
and enrich our understanding of why men did not see eye to eye
on the Constitution.

Commentary BY JACKSON TURNER MAIN

Thomas J. Archdeacon's paper is interesting, convincing, and exceptionally well written. The author should be complimented on his ability to use statistics and yet write in understandable English. This study is a good example of quantitative analysis, in which the historian, instead of relying on a few illustrations, has examined all the evidence.

It is worth noting that James A. Henretta's work on Boston indicates a very similar distribution of wealth, except that in Boston wealth was a little more concentrated. A comparison between New York and Boston—and Philadelphia as well—might pay substantial dividends. Furthermore, this broadened perspective might indicate whether newcomers with capital and connections often pushed away the previous settlers other than those who had succeeded in trade, so that the inland movement of the Dutch was really unconnected to their national origin. Comparative analysis of several cities can test this point. In addition, separate studies of the distribution of wealth among the English and the Dutch would strengthen the value of Archdeacon's work.

Edwin G. Burrows' paper is also stimulating and on the right track. The study would have been stronger had the author proceeded much further along some of the lines he indicated. The sample, for a start, is much too small for confident generalization, and suggestive only. Burrows has exaggerated the experiences of the Continental and militia soldiers. The militia was not "notoriously unreliable and inefficient," but won a number of battles, and quite a few militia companies struck telling blows for independence. One may doubt whether enlisted men in either service felt the same about their experiences as did their officers. Either the similarity must be demonstrated or the discussion limited to officers. In addition, the distinction in politics between the Continental and militia officers had been drawn earlier by Forrest McDonald and especially in William A. Benton's article on Pennsylvania.

Burrows uses the cosmopolitan-localist dichotomy imagina-

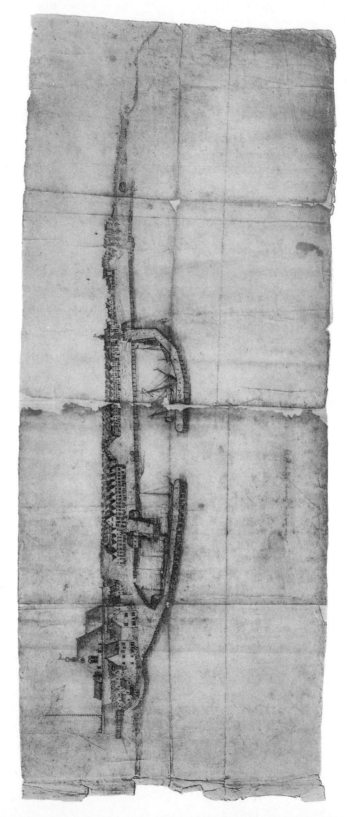

The "Labadist" view of New York, ca. 1679–1680 which accompanied the manuscript "Journal of a Voyage to New York" by Jasper Danckaerts and Peter Sluyter. The drawing and "Journal" are in the collections of the Long Island Historical Society.

tively, but it still must be demonstrated that this factor was significantly independent of other factors, and that the Continental-militia factor was an independent component of cosmopolitanism and localism. The hypothesis must be subjected to a number of tests, including the proper procedures for such analysis, the need to identify and examine all of the elements contained in these world-views, and the necessity to demonstrate the importance of this factor against correlatives such as place of residence, relative wealth, occupation, and others. One might start with New York and then, if a positive result is obtained, predict the outcome in another state and test it.

Finally, the issue of ratification was just one among many. We can understand it better by placing it in broader context. Moreover, by examining various other issues of the period we can better test the influence of many factors which affected political behavior over a period of time. The research I have just completed on political parties during the Confederation period is instructive in this regard. About 1,500 roll-call votes in seven state legislatures during the 1780's have been examined, revealing that the legislators divided into two consistent parties that may be termed "commercial-cosmopolitan" and "agrarian-localist." Biographical data on 1,500 legislators have been assembled, and the significance of various correlations analyzed. This work indicates that Burrows is correct in his basic conclusion, but there is still need for additional study of this broad subject.

The American Revolution Comes to John Jay

Richard B. Morris

For no other state among the original 13 is the controversy over the coming of the Revolution as fierce as in the case of New York. Though the work of Carl L. Becker may be found at the vortex of this historical problem, the essential question of why the colonists rebelled is still clouded by enigma. The causes of the Revolution in New York were many, the men involved acted for diverse reasons, and the special complications of city and state differences form the basis for conflicting views.

Richard B. Morris' incisive study, "The American Revolution Comes to John Jay," is especially instructive in this regard. Morris changes the focus of analysis to the individual, to a man whose impact on these events was substantial, and yet whose uncertainties about the proper course to follow with respect to Great Britain were apparent even to himself. If, in fact, the Revolution did "come" to John Jay, we can suggest further that the same pattern prevailed for countless other individuals. As in the dilemma of John Jay, the colonists made the Revolution while at the same time the Revolution profoundly changed many of them.

IF WE EVER HAD a "radical chic" in America it was in 1776, when middle-class morality discovered grounds in higher law to advocate subversion and republicanism. Representative of this elitist revolution of conservative inclinations was John Jay, a man with a deep distaste for mobbism and demagoguery, who, perhaps more than any other New Yorker, played the decisive role in swinging New York to independence. Indeed, John Jay's career embodies much of the ambivalence of the American War for Independence—the resort to revolution while insisting on justifying its legality, the appeal to force while resolving to maintain law and order.

96

Portrait of John Jay by John Trumbull in the
John Jay House, Katonah, New York.

John Jay's early drive to obtain an unassailably secure social position represents a long struggle of an outsider and his family —a family of non-English stock, chiefly French and Dutch—to obtain status and security. At King's College he early achieved a reputation as a principled and unbending young man who would stick to the letter of the law regardless of consequences—a trait which stamped his behavior thereafter whether in law, politics, or diplomacy. Among the other factors in Jay's formative years which left a lasting imprint on his personality was the rivalry with his eccentric brother Sir James, with whom competition turned to mortal antipathy; and Jay's peculiar situation as the only member of a large family to have any semblance of intellectual capacity. Thus he grew up very fast, and despite his junior position in the family in years, he assumed paternal responsibilities at an early age.

Jay got along extremely well with his peers, but his subordinates at times found him authoritarian, vain, and stuffy, a man who stiffened at slights deliberate or unintended. Jay's Spanish mission immediately comes to mind. Accompanying him to Spain in 1779 was his personal secretary and brother-in-law Henry Brockholst Livingston. Twenty-two years old when he joined Jay's official family, Brockholst had as a young army officer shown himself adept at positioning himself wherever the action might be. In Spain he was captious, sulky, ill-mannered, and spoiled. He constantly baited John Jay by making indiscreet and improper remarks highly critical of the Americans and their government. His provocative rudeness led to his dismissal, and Jay breathed a sigh of relief when Brockholst took passage for home in the spring of 1782. Back in New York, after being captured by the British on the high seas, imprisoned, and then released on parole, Brockholst joined the small group of John Jay haters. With Jay a leading Federalist, he wasted little time in joining the antis. When in 1792 John Jay put his signature to a treaty with England that bears his name, Brockholst stood in the forefront of demonstrations denouncing it. Surely it was no accident that he was present at the riot at which Hamilton was hit by a flying stone as well as on the occasion in New York when John

Jay was burned in effigy. His disaffection for Jay endeared him to the Jeffersonian camp, and President Jefferson put him on the Supreme Court, the first riot provocateur in American history to reach so exalted a station.

As Congress, not Jay, had appointed William Carmichael to the post of Secretary to the Spanish Mission, the subordinate never felt any loyalty to his chief. From the beginning of their trip abroad, Jay felt that Carmichael had launched upon a systematic intrigue to undermine the authority which the American minister plenipotentiary jealously guarded. Convivial while Jay was stand-offish, a Spanish linguist which Jay was not, Carmichael proved an acute observer of Spanish affairs. From the start he hit it off with the Spaniards as well as with the French ambassador, the Comte de Montmorin, an accomplishment which indubitably earned him poor marks in Jay's book. Jay was annoyed by the intimacy between Carmichael and Brockholst Livingston, distrusted his Secretary's discretion, questioned his handling of accounts, and took a strict view of his powers. He felt that Carmichael was jealous of him, which was no doubt true, but for his own part he was envious of his subordinate's little successes and recognized the "cloven foot" which his Secretary at first took pains to conceal. Jay's antipathy to Carmichael was, if anything, sharpened by the latter's success in Madrid after Jay went on to Paris, leaving his Secretary to act as *chargé d'affaires*. Through Lafayette's intercession, Carmichael was formally received by the Spanish king and royal family in 1783, ten days before the signing of the definitive peace, an honor not customarily accorded to any but those holding the rank of minister. It is indeed a pity that, in view of Carmichael's good standing and influence at the Spanish court to which Jay attested, Jay could not have been more forbearing of his subordinate. To the last, however, Jay was irreconcilable. When, years after the events, Jay arranged his papers, he made the following notation in the bundle of Carmichael correspondence:

Care should be taken of these papers. They include letters to and from William Carmichael—a man who mistook cunning for wisdom; and who in pursuing his purposes, preferred the guidance of artifice and simulation, to that of truth and rectitude. He finally yielded to intemperance, and died a bankrupt.

Jay's estrangement from the Establishment on the eve of the Revolution was provoked by an altercation with the Attorney General over private litigation, by his failure to secure a land grant from the governor, and by the administration's turning down a proposal that he and Robert R. Livingston, his former law partner, be appointed to the common pleas bench. At the very time when Jay was serving as a delegate to the First Continental Congress he was in correspondence with two Tory friends in London to have them pull strings to get him the judgeship.

Jay forged a link to the Whig cause by marrying the daughter of the Whig lawyer-intellectual, William Livingston, who not only was among the most prominent of the Whiggish-leaning Livingstons but was soon to supplant Tory governor William Franklin as the Revolutionary chief executive of New Jersey. But before that marriage transpired, current gossip had Jay courting two different daughters of Peter De Lancey, and marrying Sarah Livingston on the rebound in April, 1774. The acidulous Judge Thomas Jones, a diehard Royalist, put it this way: "Mr. Jay . . . took a wife . . . in the Livingston (family), a family ever opposed in politics to the De Lanceys, turned Republican, espoused the Livingston interest, and ever after opposed all legal government." Jones himself had married into the De Lancey family and seemed to speak from firsthand, but so oversimplified an explanation of Jay's political motivations as Jones's seems to warrant some modification. In any event, Jay never held his early failures as a suitor against the De Lanceys. When they became Tories and James De Lancey was captured and jailed at Hartford, Jay advanced him one hundred dollars along with the assurance that never would "the good offices formerly done by yourself and family cease to excite my gratitude."

Jay's Sally, a beautiful and gracious if somewhat shallow young woman, 11 years Jay's junior, inherited her good looks from her mother, for her father, the governor-to-be, liked to describe himself as "a long-nosed, long-chinned, ugly-looking fellow." She did not, however, inherit his brains. Bearing a striking resemblance to Marie Antoinette, although less sharp-featured, she was frequently mistaken for the Queen when in the war years she would enter a box at the Paris Opéra. Sweet-tempered and kindly, at least to her intimates, but somewhat gushy and lightheaded, Sally was considered by some people to be a haughty social climber, but in Whig circles she was in truth born at the top.

A combination of newly formed ties to the politically activist Livingston clan and an upsurge of civil unrest nudged Jay ever so gently into the opposition camp. Happily married, looking forward to a judicial post, the court dockets bulging with his cases, hobnobbing with New York's elite at the Dancing Assembly, the Debating Society, and the Moot, where bright legal minds argued legal propositions of an evening, Jay was hardly a frustrated revolutionary. In his case events took a hand. A few days before his wedding a group of radicals calling themselves "the Mohawks" dumped a cargo of tea in New York harbor as a protest against the closing of the port of Boston by act of Parliament. This disciplined demonstration provided proof of the re-emergence of the old Sons of Liberty with working-class support, and it touched off a renewed battle between radicals and conservatives for control of the protest movement. The movement came to a head when on May 12 news reached New York of the enactment by Parliament of the bill closing the port of Boston. The conservatives showed themselves adept at political maneuvering by bringing about the election of a Committee of Fifty-One, in which they had a slight majority. It is on this committee that John Jay, along with some 19 future Tories, including such friends as Edward Laight, made his initial bow in provincial politics.

Conservative or no, Jay's role as a political activist propelled him by almost imperceptible stages into a role of leadership of the revolutionary movement in New York. At the start it was as a penman that his talents were enlisted. The Committee picked him to draft a diplomatic reply to the Bostonians who had demanded complete nonintercourse with England. Jay's reply carefully sidestepped the boycott that New York merchants would have found so painful, while stressing the necessity of immediately assembling a general Congress. That latter step ultimately proved the more radical course. His reply characterized the judicial temper that was the hallmark of a John Jay paper. First, he sounded a note of caution. "What ought to be done in a situation so truly critical, while it employs the anxious thoughts of every generous mind, is very hard to be determined." Certainly a general Congress must be assembled "without delay," but pending such action, it would be "premature" to make a commitment on the "expedient" proposed by the Bostonians. Caution was still Jay's watchword. Did sponsorship of a call for the convening of a Continental Congress mean that Jay had crossed his Rubicon? Clearly not, for the very day the Committee endorsed his letter he wrote to Vardill in London reporting what had happened and indicating that he would accept a judicial post.

With conservatives maintaining a checkrein on the contagious "levelling trend" which might be picked up from New England, and after much jockeying for control between radical and moderate factions, a delegation to the first Continental Congress was elected on July 28, a delegation that included Mr. Jay. Jay's election was a victory over the radicals, who had made what Lieutenant Governor Colden described as a "Violent effort" to substitute for the moderate Jay and John Alsop the radical John Morin Scott and that "Wilkes of New York," Alexander McDougall. That so touchy a person as Jay, one so sensitive to his own reputation, could survive the factional brawling of those weeks attests to his tenacity and iron will. Along the way he did manage to pay off a score or two. He called upon John Morin Scott to justify or repudiate accusations "so black and so false" against Jay and his fellow committeemen, "as it cannot be presumed you would wantonly sport with the reputation of persons whose attachment to the interest of the country has never been questioned," Jay scolded. Scott must have his reasons, and in justice to Jay's character, he insisted on hearing them. This was the same Jay of the Randall correspondence and the Kempe exchange. Always must his reputation be fiercely guarded.

In that memorable session at Philadelphia's Carpenter Hall,

which first convened on September 5, 1774, battle lines were quickly drawn between radicals and conservatives. Jay was quickly identified with the latter bloc. His forces were defeated on the choice of a hall, defeated in their picking a secretary, preferring Silas Deane to the more openly acknowledged radical Charles Thomson of Pennsylvania, but proved their tough fiber in contesting Patrick Henry's proposal that the votes of each colony be apportioned on the basis of population. With characteristic impetuosity Henry declared: "Government is dissolved. . . . We are in a state of nature, sir." In a calm rejoinder Jay reminded the delegates that "the measure of arbitrary power is not full, and I think it must run over, before we undertake to frame a new constitution." Rather, the task was to endeavor "to correct faults in an old one." Jay gave a glimmer of the future revolutionary in conceding that the British Constitution which derived its authority "from compact" could impliedly be renounced by compact, but he still steered a cautious middle course, epitomized in a quotation John Adams attributed to him: "Negotiation, suspension of commerce, and war." War, he is reported to have said, was "by general consent to be waived at present." "I am for negotiation and suspension of commerce." While by no means agreeing with Jay, Adams in a restrospective comment on Jay's performance in the Congress conceded that he, along with Dickinson, had "eloquence" but lacked the "chaste," "pure," "nervous" style of Samuel Adams. To Adams, Jay would show himself to be "a man of wit, well-informed, a good speaker and an elegant writer." These latter talents Jay would speedily demonstrate, although the conciliatory cause that he had initially pursued earned him "a horrid opinion" in Patrick Henry's judgment, one which the Virginia Lees fully shared. Jay's arguments against proportionate voting prevailed, and the delegates decided to vote by provincial units, each province having one vote (a rule that prevailed throughout the history of the Continental Congress).

For the radicals the setback was at most a temporary one. On September 17 they succeeded in winning Congress's endorsement of the Suffolk Resolves, declaring the Intolerable Acts unconstitutional, advising the people to arm and form their own militia, and recommending stringent economic sanctions against Britain. Rebounding from this stunning defeat, Jay, Duane, and Edward Rutledge of South Carolina, along with other conciliationists, rallied behind Joseph Galloway's plan of union, levying as it did so heavily upon Franklin's Albany Plan of 1754. By the margin of a single vote that plan was defeated, and the radical forces gathered enough momentum to have the vote expunged from the record.

For the propaganda battle which Congress now proceeded to wage against Britain the most talented penmen among the moderates were enlisted. John Dickinson drew up the petition to the King when Patrick Henry's draft proved inept; and John Jay, who had perhaps grudgingly signed the Continental Association, won the acclaim of both factions for his draft of an address to the people of Great Britain. The story of that address comes to us from Jefferson secondhand. Richard Henry Lee prepared a first draft, which, when it was read, "every countenance fell and a dead silence ensued for many minutes." Then on the following day, October 19, William Livingston read the draft that his son-in-law had prepared. When it was read, as Jefferson reported it, "there was but one sentiment of admiration."

Jay's "Address to the People of Great Britain" propelled him at once into the front line of Whig propagandists and survives as proof that if you associate with radicals long enough some of the radical rhetoric is bound to rub off on you. So indeed the Tories felt, and, though Jay's role in the Continental Congress had been that of a moderate, his authorship of the "Address" and his signature on the Continental Association caused raised eyebrows among bitter-end partisans of the Ministry.

The Tories were now ready to write him off, quite prematurely in fact. "You will be surpriz'd, my dear Vardill, as well as affected," wrote William Laight to his London correspondent toward the end of March, 1775, "when I tell you of the loss of that once steady, honest Protestant Jay. He is, in the opinion of almost all of our friends, turned, in politics, a rigid Blue Skin." The only way that Laight could account for the switch was Jay's "too sudden elevation to a popular character." To Laight, Jay was obviously courting popularity, "and to please the populace he must have thrown aside his old principles." Imagine, only a few nights back, he presided over a meeting where Lamb, Sears, Garret Roorback, and other activists were the principal speakers! As further evidence of Jay's "defection," Laight cited the fact that "the Blues trumped his merits and patriotism at every corner of the streets." Once Jay had charged McDougall with demagoguery; now he applauded his zeal and supported his measures. Don't let him know how we feel, Laight counseled. Rather, congratulate him on his re-election and tell him how pleased we are to "have a writer and speaker of his abilities among us, who heretofore has, and doubtless continues to counteract the views of our ambitious, Republican demagogues. He may, and 'tis the prayer of his friends that he should, see his error." By this date there is no evidence that Jay and Vardill were any longer in communication with each other, although as late as October, 1775, William Laight, from the security of London, was writing an unsolicited letter, admonishing Jay about the prudence of being contented with "a moderate share of civil liberty" rather than of "aiming at visionary schemes of perfect freedom," which, the British army, preparing to descend upon the colonies in the spring and to "cover the face of the whole country," would most certainly crush.

Moderate though he had been in the First Congress, Jay found that his prestige had risen among the Whig activists and they in turn, as the Tories found to their chagrin, embraced him as one of their own. On his return to New York he, along with his brother Frederick, was elected to the newest extralegal governing body, the Committee of Sixty, as well as to the Committee of Inspection appointed to police compliance with the Continental Association. A stickler for the rules, Jay quickly won a reputation as a zealous inspector. Tories whispered that he informed the Sons of Liberty of the names of ladies and gentlemen who drank tea at the dancing assembly over which he presided. Various signs indicated that Jay was more and more being propelled to a position of leadership of the moderate wing of the protest movement. It was he who drafted the letter from the New York Committee of Sixty to the Committee of Boston, assuring the latter that they should have no cause for fearing "a defection" on the part of "the bulk of the people." As a moderate he still sought to have some control over citywide elections. Rather than have the election of delegates to the Provincial Convention conducted at an unsupervised mass meeting, Jay proposed that the elections be held in the wards under the supervision of the vestrymen and subcommittees of the Sixty, the voting to be confined to freeholders and freemen. The radicals conceded this point, and with their support, the slate, including John Jay, was declared duly elected.

Aside from his lawyer-like repugnance to unsupervised elections at large mass meetings, Jay made it clear that he preferred to have the delegates to the Continental Congress elected by the Provincial Convention rather than by the voters directly, a preference which he asserted again at election time the following year. That is precisely what was done. The Provincial Convention, assembling in New York City on April 20, elected a slate of delegates to the Second Continental Congress which included Jay but substituted for two conservatives men of more radical complexion. In the wild demonstration that broke out upon news of Lexington and Concord, the Committee of Sixty recommended that a Committee of One Hundred be elected with enlarged powers and that a Provincial Congress be summoned, as the Tory Assembly had already adjourned. In the enthusiasm of the moment it seemed an effortless task to secure a thousand signatures to a new Association, in whose drafting Jay was prominent, pledging obedience to all acts of the Continental and Provincial Congresses. Before Jay left for Philadelphia in early May the new governing committee commanded most of his time.

In the Second Continental Congress Jay, along with John Dickinson and Edward Rutledge, quickly assumed the leadership of the moderate wing. Still he allowed himself to be drafted to prepare a "Letter to the Oppressed Inhabitants of Canada," in the course of which he turned a complete ideological somersault. In his "Appeal" Jay had charged the British government with backing "our Roman Catholic neighbors" against the English Protestant colonists to reduce them to a form of slavery by unconstitutional taxation. Now, in seeking support from Catholic Quebec, Jay, perhaps with tongue in cheek, reminded the people of Canada that "the fate of the Protestant and Catholick Colonies" was "strongly linked together," and invited their support in breaking "the fetters of slavery."

Throughout the spring and summer of 1775 Jay continued to perform a neat balancing act, skimming along the narrow wire of conciliation while allowing himself to be utilized by the forces that were prepared for direct confrontation. The spring of 1775 marked the climax of the final conciliation effort. The hour was late. Congress, upon convening in May, learned that its petition of October, 1774 had been virtually ignored by Parliament, that the ministry intended to use troops, and that in fact a shooting war had already broken out in New England. Against the burgeoning opinion that any further conciliatory moves were fruitless, the conciliatory party in Congress centering on Jay, Duane, and John Dickinson, made one last desperate stand. The opportunity arose on May 15, when Congress adopted a resolution instructing the inhabitants of New York "to defend themselves and their property and repel force by force." It was at this time, with a view to obviating any decision that might invite attack or close the door to reconciliation, that Jay made a motion for a second petition to the King, which Dickinson seconded. To win over the war hawks the two moderates pointed out that any delay would give the colonists needed time for military preparations, while a rejection of the appeal by the home government would serve only to unite the colonies. Congress, despite the diehards, saw the force of their argument and authorized such a petition, naming Jay, along with Dickinson, Franklin, Thomas Johnson, and John Rutledge as a committee to draft it.

The petition as finally adopted is indisputably from the pen of John Dickinson, but Jay's original draft suggests how much more conciliatory he was prepared to be than his fellow committeemen. Jay asked that "every irritating measure be suspended," while Dickinson proposed the repeal of distasteful statutes. With his fondness for commissions, Jay proposed that George III "commission some good and great men to enquire into the grievances of her faithful subjects" while Dickinson contented himself with leaving it to his Majesty to "direct some mode" by which reconciliation could be achieved. Jay explicitly disavowed independence as an end, a commitment which Dickinson shrewdly sidestepped. Jay suggested that, should the royal government prefer not to deal with Congress, negotiations might be conducted with the colonial assemblies. Dickinson realized that Congress could not be expected to adopt a self-denying ordinance and avoided including the proposal, while at the same time arranging for the petition to be signed by individuals to offset the fact that it was adopted in a general Congress, a body so unpalatable to George III. In short, Dickinson's final draft scrupulously avoided ruffling the sensibilities of Congress by making injudicious and even unnecessary admissions or concessions. In view of the heated opposition in Congress to so watered-down a version as the final Olive Branch Petition, it is obvious that the Jay draft never had the slightest chance of adoption.

Still an empire man, still loyal to the King, Jay throughout the greater part of the summer and fall of 1775 was hopeful of the petition's favorable reception. As late as October 17 he wrote Alexander McDougall, "No news as to the effect of our petition. God grant it may be a means of restoring the peace and I may add the prosperity of the Empire now rent by unnatural convulsions. But we ought not to rely wholly on it, lest it prove a broken reed and pierce us." Jay's sober conclusion proved amply justified, for on November 9 Congress learned that the King had rejected the Petition.

In the weeks and months following the adoption of the Olive Branch Petition Jay found himself in an increasingly ambivalent position, very much as Congress itself, in John Adams' impatient view, was suspended "between hawk and buzzard." Even after the rejection of the Petition Jay continued to hope, vainly as it proved, for a conciliatory gesture from the Crown, and in a speech in March, 1776 criticized the wording of a privateering bill because it indicted the King as the author of colonial miseries instead of putting the onus on the Ministry.

A do-nothing policy would in the longer run be insupportable to Jay, who was by temperament an activist, a believer that government must be infused with energy. He was coming to take a Continental approach to the distribution of war powers, an approach which would not too long thereafter stamp him as a leading nationalist. Thus, he no longer believed that the states should retain the initiative in making separate proposals for conciliation, but that such matters be left to the Congress. He and his fellow delegates from New York realistically abstained from presenting to Congress a plan of accommodation adopted by the Provincial Congress of New Jersey. It was altogether fitting that he, along with such other legal rights as John Dickinson and George Wythe of Virginia, should be dispatched to Trenton by Congress to talk the New Jersey Assembly out of their plan to send their own petition to the King. He told the Jerseymen that "we had nothing to expect from the mercy or justice of Britain," that petitions were no longer the means, rather vigor and unanimity were "the only means." Only the petition of "United America presented by Congress, ought to be relied on," he insisted; all else was "unnecessary."

Whether Jay willed it or no, there was a war on, one being waged on several fronts, and it was up to the states and the Congress to carry it on effectively. Jay served on such crucial Congressional committees as the Committee of Secret Correspondence to secure aid from abroad, an assignment which provided him with a cloak-and-dagger encounter with the French secret agent Bônvouloir and an active correspondence with the American agent to France, Silas Deane, in which he used an invisible ink according to a formula provided by Jay's brother Sir James. On a committee of Congress to deal with disaffection in Queens County, he joined in drafting a report urging the arrest of subversive persons, the detention of those who voted against sending delegates to Congress, and the disarming of dissidents—in all, strong medicine for a moderate. Constantly now he prodded Patriots back in New York to begin exercising essential governmental functions. To Alexander McDougall he wrote on December 23, 1775, "It appears to me prudent that you should begin to impose light taxes, rather with a view to *precedent* than profit." He went on to suggest that saltpeter and wool might be accepted in payment, a step which would "encourage manufacture." Then, pointing out that such measures were essential "to the support of the poor," he added this revelatory comment: "It keeps people easy and quiet. By being employed they gain bread. When our Fellow Mortals are busy and well fed, they forget to complain." Learning that the Provincial Congress had issued more paper money, Jay admonished, "Will you never think of taxes? The ice must be broken, the sooner it is begun and more insensibly performed the better. I tremble for the delay." McDougall soon persuaded Jay that New York City under its existing stresses and strains should not have to bear a disproportionate share of the state's tax burdens.

Jay's reluctance to move toward independence, combined with an enthusiasm for the assertion by the Thirteen Colonies of the governmental powers of autonomous states, epitomizes his ambivalent frame of mind throughout the spring of 1776. As the groundswell for independence seemed to be carrying all before it, Jay inched toward overt resistance. At McDougall's suggestion he applied for a military commission and was duly appointed colonel of the Second Regiment, New York City militia.

During the spring of 1776 Jay's own province had first call upon his time. Elected a delegate to the New York Provincial Congress in April, Jay was not present in the Continental Congress when some of the crucial decisions of the spring and summer of 1776 were made. Thus, on May 11 James Duane wrote to apprise him that the day before Congress had adopted a momentous resolution recommending the colonies "to adopt such government as shall, in the opinion of the representatives of the people, best conduce to the happiness and safety of their constituents in particular, and Americans in general." Jay took his seat in the new Provincial Congress on May 25, and was at once placed on one committee to draft a law relating to the perils to which the colony was exposed by "its intestine dangers" and on another to act on the Congressional mandate to form a new government. On the one hand Jay was convinced that a new government must be formed as the old colonial one would "no longer work anything but mischief." On the other, he was opposed to a precipitate move toward independence.

On June 11, four days after Richard Henry Lee had offered in Congress a resolution affirming that the United Colonies "are, and of right ought to be, free and independent states," Jay moved that it was the sense of the Provincial Congress "that the good people of this colony have not, in the opinion of this congress, authorized this congress, or the delegates of the colony in the Continental Congress, to declare this colony to be and continue to be independent of the crown of Great Britain." Jay might well have made this proposal on his own initiative, but he had been constantly prodded by James Duane in Congress to see that New York did not follow the precipitate action urged by "the orators from Virginia." Jay was prepared to "take a solitary ride to Philadelphia" when he was so charged by the Provincial Congress, but since his presence was urgently needed in New York he was, perhaps conveniently, absent on July 2 when the decisive vote on independence took place in Congress. Since he did not find an opportunity to return to Congress for the rest of the year his signature was never affixed to the Declaration of Independence.

Would Jay have signed the Great Declaration had he been present in Philadelphia that summer? The signs are none too clear. Bear in mind that it was his resolution of June 11 which withheld from the New York delegates the power of voting for independence. Remember that Jay had long hoped for a conciliatory resolution of the issues between colonies and empire. Even as late as April, 1778, Jay confided to his friend Gouverneur Morris, a man of like views on many political subjects though lacking Jay's balanced judgment and prudence: "The destruction of old England would hurt me. I wish it well. It afforded my ancestors an asylum from persecution." Even at that date Jay would have been content with independence and a treaty affording the new United States commercial advantages—in other words, a negotiated peace that would let England withdraw from the war with honor. Evidently his friend Edward Rutledge felt that Jay's vote, had he been in Congress, would have been cast with "the sensible part of the house," opposing Lee's motion for independence. "I wish you had been here," he wrote on June 8 disconsolately. On the 29th he wrote again to urge that Jay attend the Congress "on Monday next" when the Declaration of Independence, a draft of the Articles of Confederation, and a scheme for a treaty with foreign powers were to be laid before the house. "Whether we shall be able effectually to oppose the first and infuse wisdom in the others will depend in a great measure upon the exertions of" what Rutledge called the "sensible part of the members." Alas, Jay could not come, as he explained in a letter of July 6. He was engaged "by plots, conspiracies, and chimeras dire." State business came first. "We have a government, you know, to form; and God only knows what it will resemble."

Jay was not only a convert to independence, but one imbued with perhaps false optimism about the cause. By July, 1776 he had assumed leadership in two areas which would irrevocably stamp him as a rebel—that of organizing the military defenses of his state and of constitution-maker. On July 2 the British launched their conquest of New York, with Sir William Howe's unopposed landing of some 10,000 troops, followed ten days later by the arrival of brother Lord Richard Howe's powerful fleet and transports, along with huge reinforcements. On July 16 the New York Convention appointed Jay to a committee charged with obstructing the channel of the Hudson River and harassing the enemy's shipping. They were authorized "to impress carriages, teams, sloops, and horses, and to call out detachments of the militia." Specifically, Jay was commissioned to secure cannon at a foundry in Salisbury, Connecticut, for Fort Montgomery in the Highlands. Jay sped over to Salisbury, learned from the proprietors that the cannon and shot could only be released by authorization of Governor Trumbull, then dashed across the mountains to Lebanon, where the governor summoned his council to act upon Jay's request. With the authorization in his pocket, Jay turned back to the Furnace, managed to round up teams to carry four twelve-pounders which were quickly made ready, then pushed across the state boundary to Livingston Manor to secure trucks and shot from Colonel Gilbert Livingston. On his return journey he overtook the convoy of cannon and shot moving toward Colonel Hoffman's Landing, and was able to oversee the cargo being put aboard ship for transport across the river to Fort Montgomery—a triumphantly breathless journey which Jay managed to record in a surviving diary fragment.

Thus the Revolution came to Jay rather than vice versa. When his commitment was made he entered into the cause with all the zealotry of a recent convert. No appeasement for him even when the hour seemed darkest. Howe's forces were readying for the amphibious landing on Long Island and the Battle of New York was soon to follow. The British threat to Westchester forced Jay's elderly parents from their home at Rye to a retreat in Fishkill. Jay joined them when the New York Convention was forced to find safety, one step ahead of the Redcoats, first in White Plains, then in Poughkeepsie, and then across the Hudson at Kingston.

In short, from a wishy-washy appeaser Jay had been transformed into a hard-line insurgent. As early as the spring of 1776 he had counseled McDougall as to the expediency of removing to less sensitive places "such as are notoriously disaffected." Already on June 16, prior to Howe's appearance, the Convention on Jay's motion had prescribed the death penalty of treason for those giving aid or comfort to the enemy. Jay was made chairman of a Committee to Detect Conspiracies, with power to seize, try, and sentence disaffected persons. The Committee held daily sittings until the arrival of the British fleet sent them scurrying. The committee investigated an alleged plot against the life of Washington, sentenced Thomas Hickey, one of Washington's soldiers to be hanged, and threw Mayor David Matthews into jail, along with 13 other disaffected persons, aside from a sizable number who were banished.

Late in September Jay was put on a reorganized committee which operated out of Fishkill. This committee was authorized not only to stamp out disaffection but to call out the militia to

suppress counterrevolutionary activities, to make drafts on the
state treasury, and to raise and officer 220 men to use as they
saw fit. Sitting at Conner's tavern in Fishkill, the committee day
after day examined prisoners under guard. Minutes of the hear-
ings were kept by Jay, who, besides acting as secretary, assumed
the permanent chairmanship after a few meetings. The suspects
were interrogated and then asked to take the oath of allegiance
to Congress. When they refused, Jay, with that stern sense of
duty of a Roman patriot, sentenced them to be jailed, trans-
ported to New Hampshire, or allowed to remain at home under
parole. Some of those sentenced were good friends like Jay's
classmate Peter Van Schaack whom he sent to Boston on parole.
Jay's inexorable performance of unpleasant duties earned him
the vituperation of the enemy. Major John André attacked him
in Rivington's *Royal Gazette* as "remarkable for a mixture of the
lowest cunning and the most unfeeling barbarity" and for en-
forcing statutes "that destroyed every species of private property
and repose."

By recent criteria André's censure was far off the mark. Jay
was no Saint-Just. A sense of fairness, a strong humanitarian im-
pulse, and a vigilant concern for the maintenance of civil liberties and due process tempered his rulings toward the disaffected. In defending his treatment of Van Schaack, Jay asserted
toward the end of the war: "I have adhered to certain fixed principles, and faithfully obeyed their dictates without regarding the
consequence of my conduct to my friends, my family, or myself."
Van Schaack chivalrously conceded that he had been treated
justly. Jay distinguished between Tories who had acted an honorable part and those whom he deemed despicable. To Van
Schaack, a refugee in England in 1782, he confessed, "I considered all who were not with us, and you among the rest, as
against us; yet be assured that John Jay did not cease to be a
friend to Peter Van Schaack." To Colonel James De Lancey, a
prisoner of war in Hartford jail, he sent a hundred dollars so
that his situation might "be comfortable and easy," but when in
postwar London he encountered Colonel Peter De Lancey, who

commanded the lawless Tory cowboys of Cooper's *The Spy*, he cut him dead.

To ferret out hidden enemies Jay organized an intelligence operation, and one of his most trusted agents who reported to Jay's secret committee was Enoch Crosby, the original for Harvey Birch, hero of James Fenimore Cooper's *The Spy*, for whom Jay years later, as Cooper acknowledged, supplied the main outlines.

Jay, like Hamilton, was deeply concerned that the administration of the loyalty oath program should remain in the hands of civilians and not be assumed by the military. "To impose a test is a sovereign act of legislation," he remonstrated to McDougall, "and when the army become our legislators, the people that moment become slaves." Along like lines he deplored such acts of mobbism as Isaac Sears' "valorous expedition" against Rivington's printing establishment. Such actions Jay considered an affront to the "honor of the colony," not to speak of the liberty of the press, and one which should not for an instant be tolerated. "The tenderness shewn to some wild people on account of their supposed attachment to the cause has been of disservice," he admonished. "The eccentric behavior has, by passing unreproved, gained countenance, lessened your authority and diminished that dignity so essential to give weight and respect to your ordinances."

When the revolutionary legislature turned to the adoption of a constitution for the new state, Jay seemed an obvious choice for a select drafting committee. Work on it was interrupted by Jay's more compelling duties in fortifying the Hudson, checking subversion, and running an intelligence service, but by March, 1777 a draft in Jay's hand was submitted to the Provincial Congress. Jay's draft underwent minor amendments and alterations, mainly introduced by Jay himself, along with Duane, Gouverneur Morris, and Robert R. Livingston.

Elitist though he was, Jay recognized how essential popular participation was to the stability of republican government. He would have extended the franchise to all who had paid both state and county taxes—a proposal very close to universal manhood suffrage. During the debates over the draft he succeeded in having voting by ballot substituted for the viva-voce method of electing representatives, and provided a means whereby illiterate voters could indicate their choices. All in all, his constitutional innovations, motions, and amendments hardly support the anti-democratic label that historians have attached to his name.

One of Jay's most significant efforts was his endeavor to have a clause inserted into the Constitution of 1777 forbidding the continuation of slavery, an institution which he abhorred. He was to become president of the New York Manumission Society in the postwar period, and his sons were later renowned leaders of the antislavery movement. In light of his lifetime aversion to slavery, it was fitting and proper that during Jay's term as governor of New York he was to affix his signature to a bill providing for the end of slavery in the state.

Appropriately, the Convention rewarded Jay for his heroic labors on the new constitution by electing him the state's Chief Justice, a post far more elevated than the one he had sought from the Crown scarce three years before. Finding judicial duties more congenial than executive ones, Jay accepted, declining to have his name advanced for the governorship. Although the cases before him did not concern large constitutional questions, Jay went out of his way to criticize the impressment of horses, teams, and carriages "by the military, without the intervention of a civil magistrate" as violative of due process of law, and urged the legislation to curb this "extraordinary power." Again, as a member of the Council of Revision, he wrote the veto of an excess profits tax levied upon war profiteers on the ground that it was violative of the equal protection of the law to which all citizens were entitled.

In short, Jay brought to his revolutionary commitment a deep concern for civil liberty, property rights, and a sense of justice rooted in the English constitutional system. An empire man and a moderate, he had traveled the long road by the winter of 1776–77. At the nadir of the Patriots' military hopes he stirred the delegates to the New York Convention with an address "to their constitutents" which they enthusiastically adopted before the heartening news of the Trenton victory and which the Continental Congress ordered translated into German. In words that might have come out of Tom Paine's contemporary *American Crisis* pamphlet, Jay declared: "We do not fight for a few acres of land, but for freedom—for the freedom and happiness of millions yet unborn." To Jay and to the other Founding Fathers these words were no mere rhetorical outpouring. Now embattled in a struggle not of his choosing, Jay felt that the fight must go on until independence was achieved. "War must make peace for us," he was to tell John Adams, "and we shall always find well-appointed armies to be our ablest negotiators."

Gone were the ambiguities, the hesitancies, the political trimming. Jay now stood at the center of the great events of the Revolutionary and early national years, a committed nationalist, an agitator for energetic government, whose career exemplifies that very special kind of revolutionary mentality that was the stamp of men of wealth and talent in New York who shared a common dream while declining to stoop to demagoguery or extremism to achieve its fulfillment.

TRUSTEES OF KINGSTON, N. Y., 1711–1776

Name	Years on Board of Trustees	Occupation	Other Offices	Assessments
Masten, Cornelius (? –1712)	1711			
Wynkoop, Evert (dates unknown)	1711, '17, '18 (3)*	brewer [?]	Supervisor (1713, '14) / Justice of Peace (1729)	£105 (1712) / £120 (1717)
Janse[n], Mattyse (? –1727)	1711, '26 (2)	shoemaker	Militia Quartermaster (1700) / Supervisor (1714) / Justice of Peace (1715, '24)	£50 (1712) / £75 (1717)
Tappen, Teunis (? –1727)	1711		Militia Ensign (1700)	£40 (1712) / £40 (1717)
Traphagen, Hendrick (dates unknown)	1711			£30 (1712)
DeLametter, Cornelius (dates unknown)	1711, '13, '14, '17-'19, '21, '23-'25, '30 (11)	tanner-shoemaker	Supervisor (1733, '34, '46) / Justice of Peace (1741, '52)	£30 (1712) / £45 (1717) / £90 (1738)
Davenport, Jan (dates unknown)	1711-'13, '19-'22, '24, '30-'37 (16)	tailor		£10 (1712) / £5 (1717)
Eltinge, William (1685-1743)	1711, '15, '16, '18, '19, '21, '23-'26	yeoman-carpenter	Supervisor (1730-'32)	£15 (1712) / £25 (1717) / In 1743 valued total estate at £489.
Post, Jan (dates unknown)	1711 (1)		Supervisor (1712)	£25 (1712) / £40 (1717)

*Total years served. Where totals not given, service started before 1711.

Name	Years on Board of Trustees	Occupation	Other Offices	Assessments	
Eltinge, Roeloff (1678–1747)	1711, '13, '14 (3)*	yeoman-tanner landowner (528 + acres)	Supervisor (1711, '25) Justice of Peace (1721) Highway Commissioner (1738)	£40 (1712) £45 (1717)	Moved to New Paltz in 1720.
Van Wagoner, Aert (1675– ?)	1711, '13–'15 (4)		Highway Commissioner (1731)	£60 (1712) £55 (1717)	Also owned lands at Hurley.
Wynkoop, Johannes, Sr. (dates unknown)	1712–'15, '19–'21 (7)		Justice of Peace (1693) Militia Major (1712) Supervisor (1717–'21, '27, '28)	£100 (1712) £115 (1717)	
Hardenbergh, Johannis (? –1748)	1712 (1)	gentleman-landowner	Sheriff (1690, 1709) Justice of Peace (1724, '41, '42) Militia Major	£100 (1712) £180 (1717)	Also owned lands at Hurley, and in Hardenbergh Patent.
Vandenbergh, Geysbert (dates unknown)	1712, '13, '23–'25, '29, '30 (7)		Militia Adjutant	£40 (1712) £50 (1717)	
Heermans, Henricus (1681– ?)	1712, '13			£10 (1712) £8 (1717)	
Hoffman, Nicholas (1680–1750)	1712, '20–'25, '37	yeoman-miller	Militia Captain (1715)	£45 (1712) £45 (1717)	Also owned lands and mill in Dutchess County.
Mattison, Tierck (1682–1742)	1712, '13, '15, '16 (4)	blacksmith-landowner		£35 (1712) £70 (1717)	
Schepmoes, William (1684–1750)	1712–'14, '20–'22 (6)	yeoman		£15 (1712) £30 (1717) £46 (1729)	
Tappen, Christophel (1681–1740)	1712, '13, '17, '18, '27–'29, '32–'36, '39, '40 (14)		Justice of Peace (1736)	£5 (1712) £25 (1717)	

*Total years served. Where totals not given, service started before 1711.

[120]   *Appendix*

Name	Years on Board of Trustees	Occupation	Other Offices	Assessments
Wynkoop, Gerrit (dates unknown)	1713 (1)*		Militia Ensign (1740)	£70 (1712)
Kiersted, Aldert (1685–1748)	1713, '16, '17, '22, '23, '25 (6)	farmer		£100 (1712) £105 (1717)
Pruyn, Hendrick (? –1752)	1714, '15, '20–'23, '25 (7)			£35 (1712) £50 (1717)
Beekman, Henry, Jr. (1688–1776)	1714 (1)	gentleman-landowner	Justice of Peace (1693–) Militia Colonel (Dutchess Co.) Assemblyman, Dutchess County (1725–1758)	Beekman's main base was in Dutchess County.
Crooke, John, Sr. (1689–1737)	1714–'16, '22, '23, '27–'29 (8)	shopkeeper-merchant	Supervisor (1722–'24)	£70 (1712) £110 (1717)
Janse[n], Hendrick (dates unknown)	1714, '15, '17–'20, '22, '24, '32, '37 (10)	yeoman		£20 (1712) £20 (1717)
Rutsen, John (? –1725)	1714, '23 (2)		Militia Captain (1715) Supervisor (1717) Justice of Peace (1724)	
Roosa, Aldert (1672[?]– ?)	1714 (1)	yeoman	Militia Sgt. (1715) Highway Comm. (1731)	£60 (1712) £55 (1717) Moved to Hurley where owned lands with brother.
Ten Broeck, Jacob, Sr. (1688– ?)	1714–'16, '19, '21, '27–'31 (9)	landowner	Justice of Peace (1741)	£440 (1712; joint assessment with brother). £215 (1717)
Ten Broeck, Johannis (1686– ?)	1715, '16, '18, '21, '24, '26–'29, '32–'36, '38–'43 (20)	farmer	Militia Captain (1738) Highway Comm. (1749)	£440 (1712; joint assessment with brother). £212 (1717)

*Total years served. Where totals not given, service started before 1711.

Name	Years on Board of Trustees	Occupation	Other Offices	Assessments
Masten, Johannis (1678– ?)	1715, '16, '25, '29–'31 (6)*	weaver		£25 (1712) £54 (1738)
Tappen, Peter (dates unknown)	1715, '20, '22–'24 (5)	brewer	Militia Sgt. (1715)	£40 (1712) £35 (1717)
Van Keuren, Matys (1681– ?)	1715 (1)			£45 (1717)
Elmendorph, Coenradt (1669–1749)	1716–'18, '37 (4)	yeoman	Sheriff [years?] Militia Captain (1700) Militia Major (1729) Justice of Peace (1724, '49)	£70 (1712) Owned additional £130 (1717) land at Hurley.
Lachair, Jan (dates unknown)	1716, '17			£25 (1712) £25 (1717)
Whitaker, James (1674– ?)	1716, '17, '26 (3)	yeoman		£115 (1712) £170 (1717)
Heermans, Andrew (1685– ?)	1716–'19, '21, '23, '26 (7)			£10 (1712) £17 (1717)
Low, Abraham (1683– ?)	1716, '17, '19, '26–'28, '30, '34–'36, '38–'43 (16)		Militia Lieutenant (1738)	£35 (1712) £55 (1717)
De Witt, Boudwyne, Jr. (dates unknown)	1717–'19, '21, '22, '25–'27, '30, '31, '33, '34 (12)			No assessment listed; father's estate seized for debt in 1703.
Legg, William, Jr. (? –1730)	1717, '27–'29 (4)	yeoman		£190 (1717)

*Total years served. Where totals not given, service started before 1711.

Name	Years on Board of Trustees	Occupation	Other Offices	Assessments	
Low, Johannis (dates unknown)	1718, '19, '29, '30, '35, '36 (6)*			£40 (1717)	
Newkirk, Arie (dates unknown)	1718 (1)	farmer	Militia Sgt. (1738)	£10 (1712) £57 (1717)	
Van Vliet, Arie (dates unknown)	1718 (1)	farmer	Militia Corporal (1715) 3rd Corporal of Militia (1738)	£10 (1712) £25 (1717)	
Ten Broeck, Wessel, Jr. (1672–1744)	1719 [refused to serve]	yeoman	Militia Captain (1712) Highway Comm. (1722) Militia Lt. Col. (1728–'38) Justice of Peace (1729)	£330 (1712) £350 (1717)	
Van Keuren, Tierck (1682–1742)	1719, '25, '26, '38–'41 (7)	blacksmith-landowner	Militia Captain (1738)	£64 (1729) £68 (1738)	Also owned lands and mill in Dutchess County.
Cantine, Peter (1693– ?)	1720, '22, '25 (3)		Highway Comm. (1755)	£12 (1717)	Had moved to Marbletown by 1728. Family one of twelve patentees at New Paltz.
Demeyer, Nicholas (1683–1769)	1720 (1)	farmer-yeoman		£35 (1717) £123 (1729)	Demeyer's will, signed with his mark, bequeathed 16 slaves to heirs.
Slecht, Anthony (1690– ?)	1720, '22, '34, '35 (4)		Supervisor (1748)	£65 (1717)	
Van Bentschoten, John (dates unknown)	1720 (1)			No assessment listed.	
Vielle, Philip (dates unknown)	1720–'22, '27, '28 (5)	artisan		£55 (1712) £50 (1717)	Probably arrived at Kingston in 1715.

*Total years served. Where totals not given, service started before 1711.

Name	Years on Board of Trustees	Occupation	Other Offices	Assessments
De Witt, Bastian (dates unknown)	1722, '28 (2)*			£25 (1712) £30 (1717)
Slecht, Jan (1694– ?)	1722, '24, '26–'28, '35, '38–'44 (13)		Militia Lieutenant (1738) Militia Captain (1749) Justice of Peace (1741)	£15 (1717) £35 (1738)
Van Buren, Tobias (1687– ?)	1723, '26, '42–'44 (5)		Militia Sgt. (1738)	£20 (1717)
Davis, Solomon (dates unknown)	1724 (1)			
Harris, William (dates unknown)	1724 (1)			£20 (1717)
Tappen, Juryan (1696– ?)	1724, '37, '38 (3)	merchant		£54 (1738)
Du Bois, Mattys (1679– ?)	1725 (1)			£125 (1712) £190 (1717) A descendant of one of original New Paltz patentees.
Turck, Johannis (1687– ?)	1725, '26, '31–'33 (5)	schoolmaster [?]		
Whitaker, Edward (? –1745)	1726 (1)	yeoman	Supervisor (1711, '16) Militia Capt. (1715–'41) Justice of Peace (1724, '41)	£115 (1712) £115 (1717)
Dumont, Jan Baptiste (1670–1749)	1727 (1)	farmer	Militia Quartermaster (1715) Highway Comm. (1738, '42)	£50 (1712) £45 (1717)

*Total years served. Where totals not given, service started before 1711.

Name	Years on Board of Trustees	Occupation	Other Offices	Assessments
DeLametter, Johannis (1697–1758)	(12)* 1727–'29, '34–'36, '38–'43	shoemaker	2nd Quartermaster of Militia (1738) Justice of Peace (1741, '52)	£27 (1738)
Swart, Tunis A. (dates unknown)	(4) 1727, '30, '32, '44	carpenter	Militia Corporal (1738)	£8 (1717) £10 (1729) £13 (1738)
Van Benschoten, Solomon (? –1737)	(10) 1728–'37	farmer [?]		£15 (1717) £100 (1738)
Plough, William (? –1735)	(2) 1728, '29	cooper		£22 (1729)
Janse[n], Johannis (1696–1792)	(20) 1729–'31, '35, '36, '38–'47, '59–'63	shoemaker	Justice of Peace (1736) Assemblyman (1747–'58)	£30 (1738)
Slecht, Johannis, Sr. (dates unknown)	(4) 1729, '31, '34, '36			
Kiersted, Hans (1677–1759)	(2) 1730, '31	doctor	Supervisor (1706)	£40 (1712) £45 (1717)
Dumont, Igonas (1701– ?)	(6) 1730–'34, '36		Militia Ensign (1738)	£1 (1729)
Snyder, Jury (dates unknown)	(4) 1730–'33	masoner	Militia Sgt. (1738)	£5 (1729) £10 (1738)
Bogardus, Petrus (1691– ?)	(18) 1731–'33, '35–'43, '52–'56, '59	blacksmith	Militia Lt. (1738)	£5 (1717) £13 (1729)

*Total years served. Where totals not given, service started before 1711.

Name	Years on Board of Trustees	Occupation	Other Offices	Assessments
Beekman, Thomas (dates unknown)	1732-'34, '38-'41 (7)*	joiner		£10 (1712), £10 (1717), £18 (1729), £20 (1738)
Du Bois, Louis M. (1677- ?)	1732, '33 (2)			£100 assessment at New Paltz (1717). Son of one of original New Paltz patentees. Lived last 10 years of life at Kingston.
DeLametter, David (1701-1769)	1732-'36, '38-'50, '52-'55 (22)	shoemaker-farmer		£10 (1729), £44 (1738)
Smedes, Petrus (1701-1783)	1734-'36, '53 (4)	miller	Militia Corporal (1738)	£5 (1729), £18 (1738)
Plough, Jan (dates unknown)	1737 (1)			£20 (1712), £80 (1717)
Schoonmaker, Hendrick H. (1694- ?)	1737 (1)		Militia Lt. (1715), Militia Captain (1738)	£11, Kingston; £25 Rochester (1729), £53 Kingston (1738)
Salisbury, Lawrence (dates unknown)	1737 (1)	farmer	Justice of Peace (1752)	£56 Foxhall (1738)
Swart, Johannis (dates unknown)	1737 (1)	carpenter		
Dumont, Johannis (dates unknown)	1738-'40 (3)		Supervisor (1737-'40)	£6 (1729), £15 (1738)
Wynkoop, Johannis [II] (1702-1791)	1738-'50 (13)	shoemaker	Supervisor (1742-'44)	£8 (1729), £44 (1738), £3 (1729)

*Total years served. Where totals not given, service started before 1711.

Name	Years on Board of Trustees	Occupation	Other Offices	Assessments	
Livingston, Gilbert (1690–1746)	1740, '41 (2)*	gentleman	County Clerk (1720's & 1730's), Assemblyman, Livingston Manor, (1728–'37), Supervisor (1740, '41, '44, '45)	£50 (1712), £36 (1738)	Son of proprietor of Livingston Manor.
Eltinge, William [II] (1713– ?)	1740, '41, '43 (3)	turner			
Elmendorph, Cornelius (1697–1792)	1742–'52 (11)	blacksmith (1759), yeoman (1784)	Militia Major (1729), Militia Quartermaster (1738)	£131 (1729), £22 (1738)	
Hoffman, Anthony (1711–1784)	1742, '43, '45–'47, '49, '51, '55–'58, '65, '69–'76 (20)	blacksmith	Supervisor (1752)	£1½ (1738)	
Wynkoop, Evert, Jr. (dates unknown)	1742, '44–'50, '52–'56 (13)	brewer	Supervisor (1749–'56), Militia Captain (1757)	£25 (1738)	
DeLametter, Jacobus (1705– ?)	1744 (1)	wheelwright	Militia Sgt. (1738)	£5 (1729), £28 (1738)	
Heermans, Jan [II] (1703– ?)	1744–'46 (3)	weaver		£6 (1729)	
De Witt, Henry (1714–1753)	1744–'48, '51 (6)	farmer (1742–'46), merchant (1752)	County Treasurer [year?]	£1 (1738)	
Persen, Cornelius (1712–1769)	1744–'53, '59–'61, '63, '64 (15)	tailor		£8 (1738)	
Crooke, John, Jr. (1711– ?)	1745–47 (3)		County Clerk (1746), Supervisor (1745, '53, '54)	£110 (1717), £122 (1738)	

*Total years served. Where totals not given, service started before 1711.

Name	Years on Board of Trustees	Occupation	Other Offices	Assessments
Hoogteling, Wilhelmus, Jr.	(23)* 1745-'50, '57-'73	farmer	Militia Lt. (1757) Justice of Peace (1762) Highway Comm. (1766)	
Van Keuren, Abraham (1711- ?)	(8) 1745-'52	blacksmith	Supervisor (1747-'51, '58-'64, '70, '71, '73, '75)	
Masten, Cornelius (1703-1787)	(4) 1748-'51	shoemaker	Militia Lt. (1773)	£21 (1738)
Dumont, Pieter (1703- ?)	(12) 1748-'52, '57-'63	masoner		£1 (1738)
Janse[n], Cornelius (1713- ?)	(9) 1758-'66	shoemaker	Militia Drummer (1738)	
Schepmoes, Dirck (dates unknown)	(1) 1748	farmer (1744) weaver (1747)		
Person, Adam (1705- ?)	(11) 1749-'51, '53, '57-'59, '62, '70-'72	tailor		£¼ (1729) £4 (1738)
Eltinge, Jacobus (dates unknown)	(5) 1750, '55-'57, '59	turner		
Du Bois, Johanris (1706-1787)	(13) 1751, '60-'64, '66-68, '70-'73	cooper		DuBois' will, dated 1772, valued estate at £350, to be divided among his eleven children.
Elmendorph, Petrus Ed. (1715-1765)	(7) 1751-'56, '59	merchant	Militia Adjutant [year?] Supervisor (1755-'56, '59-'65) Deputy County Clerk (1761) Surrogate (1762)	

* Total years served. Where totals not given, service started before 1711.

Name	Years on Board of Trustees	Occupation	Other Offices	Assessments
Eltinge, Jan (? –1762)	1751, '53–'56 (5)*	schoolmaster (1739) turner (1747) merchant (1759)	Supervisor (1746, '57) Surrogate (1760)	£6 (1738)
Hasbrouck, Abraham (1707–1791)	1752 (1)	merchant	Supervisor (1747, '57) Assemblyman (1739–'52, '59–'68) Militia Lt. Col. [years?]	£16 (1738) A very wealthy merchant. Left to heirs land, several thousand pounds, bonds, mortgages, & many slaves.
Slecht, Benjamin (dates unknown)	1752–'54 (3)	cooper		
Ten Broeck, Jacob, Jr. (1724–1793)	1753, '58 (2)	farmer		
Bruyn, Severyn (1726–1759)	1753, '58 (2)	merchant	Supervisor (1758)	
Masten, Benjamin (dates unknown)	1754, '56, '67, '68, '71 (6)	weaver		
Slecht, Johannis, Jr. (1719–1791)	1754–'73 (20)	brewer	Justice of Peace (1762)	
Snyder, Johannis, Jr. (1720– ?)	1754–'68, '70–'72 (18)		Justice of Peace (1762, '69) Supervisor (1771–'73) Militia Lt. (1757) Militia Lt. Col. (1776)	Left a moderate estate, including a few cows & sheep & ¼ share of a tan mill.
Van Buren, Cornelius (1715–1770)	1754–'56 (3)	shoemaker	Militia Capt. (1759) Highway Comm. (1766)	
Swart, Adam (dates unknown)	1756–'58, '60–'63, '66–'68, '70 (11)	carpenter		

*Total years served. Where totals not given, service started before 1711.

Name	Years on Board of Trustees	Occupation	Other Offices	Assessments
Whitaker, Edward, Jr. (dates unknown)	1757 (1)*	farmer	Justice of Peace (1752) Militia 2nd Lt. (1775)	
Dumont, Philip (dates unknown)	1757 (1)	farmer		
Elmendorph, Gerrit (1696– ?)	1757, '58 (2)	farmer	Militia 2nd Corp. (1738)	£96 (1738)
Low, Cornelius (1724– ?)	1757, '58 (2)			
Beekman, John (dates unknown)	1758, '69, '72, '74–'76 (6)	gunsmith		
Elsworth, William (dates unknown)	1759–'66, '69, '76 (10)		Militia Sgt. (1757)	
Slecht, Hendrick (dates unknown)	1759–'69, '74–'76 (14)		Militia Lt. (1761)	
De Witt, Andries F. (1728–1806)	1760–'69 (10)	farmer	County Coroner (1758) Supervisor (1772) Highway Comm. (1772) Militia Lt. Col. (1775)	
Slecht, Abraham (dates unknown)	1760–'64 (5)	tailor		
Jansen, Henry (dates unknown)	1764–'65 (2)	farmer	Militia Lt. (1758)	

*Total years served. Where totals not given, service started before 1711.

Name	Years on Board of Trustees	Occupation	Other Offices	Assessments
Masten, Ezekiel (1725–1789)	1764–'68, '70, '71, '73 (8)*	shoemaker		
Wynkoop, Derick, Jr. (1731–1796)	1764–'76 (13)	merchant	Militia Lt. (1761) Justice of Peace (1762, '69) Supervisor (1765–'69)	
Plough, Paulus (dates unknown)	1755, '66, '70 (3)	cooper		
Schoonmaker, Edward (dates unknown)	1765 (1)	farmer	Militia 1st Lt. (1775)	
DeLametter, Abraham, Jr. (dates unknown)	1766 (1)			
Low, Abraham, Jr. (dates unknown)	1767–'69 (3)		Sheriff (1746–'53) Supervisor (1766–'70, '75, '76)	
Tappen, Christopher (dates unknown)	1767–'76 (10)		Deputy County Clerk (1759–1812) Militia Major (1775)	
Elmendorph, Jonathan (1723–1798)	1769, '74–'76 (4)	farmer	Militia Major (1775)	
Van Gaasbeck, Abraham (dates unknown)	1769–'75 (7)	skipper		
Gasherie, Joseph (dates unknown)	1771–'76 (6)		Coroner (1758) Surrogate (1766)	

*Total years served. Where totals not given, service started before 1711.

Name	Years on Board of Trustees	Occupation	Other Offices	Assessments
Low, Benjamin (? –1796)	1772, '74–'76 (4)*	barber	Militia Capt. (1757)	
Persen, Johannis (1737–1800)	1772 (1)	tailor	Militia Ensign (1775)	
Salisbury, Sylvester (dates unknown)	1773–'76 (4)		Militia 1st Lt. (1775)	
Eltinge, William, [Jr.?] (1713– ?)	1774, '75 (2)	turner		
Van Gaasbeck, Jacobus (dates unknown)	1774–'76 (3)			
Van Keuren, Johannis (dates unknown)	1776 (1)	carpenter		

*Total years served. Where totals not given, service started before 1711.

Chart is based on material from: Ulster County Assessment Lists, Town of Kingston, 1712, Jan. 23, 1717, Feb. 11, 1729, 1738; Highway Commission Records, Ulster County Records, Reel 1, micro.; Grand Jury Lists, Reels 1, 5, 27, micro.; Historical Documents Collection, Queens College. Misc. MSS, Kingston, and Ulster County, New-York Historical Society; "Records of the Town Court, Proceedings of the Trustees, etc. of Kingston, Oct. 7, 1713–Feb., 1737," NYHS; Gustave Anjou, comp., *Ulster County, N. Y., Probate Records in the Office of the Surrogate and in the County Clerk's Office at Kingston, N. Y.*, 2 vols. (New York, privately printed, 1906); E. B. O'Callaghan, comp., *Calendar of New York Colonial Commissions* (New York, 1929); *Olde Ulster* (Ulster County Historical Society, 1904–1914), 10 Vols.; Marius Schoonmaker, *The History of Kingston, New York* (New York, 1888); : W. Poucher and Byron J. Terwilliger, *Old Gravestones of Ulster County, New York*, Ulster County Hist. Soc. Colls., I (1931).

NOTES

Milton M. Klein (pages 8–28)

1. Nathan Glazer and Daniel P. Moynihan, *Beyond the Melting Pot* (Cambridge, Mass., 1963), p. 2.
2. Wesley F. Craven, *The Legend of the Founding Fathers* (New York, 1956; Ithaca, 1965), Chapter 1.
3. Jeremy Belknap, *History of New Hampshire* (1812), III, 172; and Samuel Williams, *Natural and Civil History of Vermont* (1798), I, 7; both quoted in Arthur Shaffer, "The Shaping of a National Tradition: Historical Writing in America: 1783–1820" (unpublished Ph.D. dissertation, UCLA, 1966), pp. 69, 133.
4. *History of the Rise, Progress and Establishment of the Independence of the United States of America* (1789), I, 72; quoted in David D. Van Tassel, *Recording America's Past* (Chicago, 1960), pp. 38–39.
5. Edward N. Saveth, *American Historians and European Immigrants, 1875–1925* (New York, 1948), pp. 34–40.
6. Allan H. Spear, "Marcus Lee Hansen and the Historiography of Immigration," *Wisconsin Magazine of History*, XLIV (1961), 258–68, esp. 266.
7. John T. Fiske, *The Dutch and Quaker Colonies*, 2 vols. (Boston, 1899); Thomas J. Wertenbaker, *The Founding of American Civilization: The Middle Colonies* (New York, 1938); Daniel G. Brinton Thompson, *Gateway to a Nation: the Middle Atlantic States and their Influence on the Development of the Nation* (Rindge, N. H., 1956). The latter is the only book, other than works on individual states, in the category "Middle Atlantic States" in the massive *Guide to the Study of the United States of America*, Roy F. Basler and others, eds. (Washington, 1960). The American Historical Association's *Guide to Historical Literature* (New York, 1961) has only Wertenbaker's book indexed under "Middle Atlantic states" [*sic*]. John Bach McMaster was one of the few historians who, in their comprehensive accounts of American development, treated the Middle Colonies with any degree of adequacy. See Eric F. Goldman, *John Bach McMaster: American Historian* (Philadelphia, 1943), pp. 79, 100–01, 133–34; and the same author's "Middle States Regionalism and American Historiography: A Suggestion," in his *Historiography and Urbanization: Essays in American History in Honor of W. Stull Holt* (Baltimore, 1941), pp. 215, 219.
8. Richard H. Shryock, "The Middle Atlantic Area in American History," *Proceedings* of the American Philosophical Society, CVIII (April, 1964), 147–55, esp. 153. See also his "Philadelphia and the Flowering of New England . . .," *Pennsylvania Magazine of History and Biography*, LXIV (1940), 305–13; and "Historical Traditions in Philadelphia and in the Middle Atlantic Area . . .," *ibid.*, LXVII (1943), pp. 115–41.
9. The latter thesis appears in John M. Head, *A Time to Rend* (Madison, Wisc., 1968), esp. pp. xiii–xiv.

10. "Problems in American History" (1892), in Everett E. Edwards, comp., *The Early Writings of Frederick Jackson Turner* (Madison, Wisc., 1938), pp. 78–79.
11. "The Significance of the Frontier in American History" (1893), *ibid.*, pp. 217–18.
12. "The Development of American Society" (1908), in Wilbur R. Jacobs, ed., *Frederick Jackson Turner's Legacy: Unpublished Writings in American History* (San Marino, Calif., 1965), p. 177.
13. "Some Sociological Aspects of American History" (1895), in *ibid.*, pp. 163–64; *The United States, 1830–1850* (New York, 1935; Gloucester, Mass., 1958), pp. 92, 94, 112, 138, 143. See also *Rise of the New West* (New York, 1906), pp. 29–30.
14. Woodrow Wilson, "Mr. Goldwin Smith's 'Views' on Our Political History," *The Forum*, XVI (1893–94), 489–99, esp. 494–96; "The Proper Perspective of American History," *ibid.*, XIX (1895), 544–59, esp. 544–46; "The Course of American History," New Jersey Historical Society *Collections* VIII (1900), 183–206, esp. 186–89. See also Louis M. Sears, "Woodrow Wilson," in William T. Hutchinson, ed., *The Marcus W. Jernegan Essays in American Historiography* (Chicago, 1937), pp. 116–17.
15. Thompson, *Gateway to a Nation*, p. 20; David M. Ellis, "New York and Middle Atlantic Regionalism," *New York History*, XXXV (1954), 5.
16. E. B. O'Callaghan, ed., *Documentary History of the State of New York*, 4 vols. (Albany, 1849–51), IV, 21; Rev. Andrew Burnaby, *Travels through the Middle Settlements in North America in the Years 1759 and 1760*, 3rd ed., Rufus R. Wilson, ed. (New York, 1904), p. 117.
17. Henry H. Kessler and Eugene Rachlis, *Peter Stuyvesant and His New York* (New York, 1959), pp. 179–86; Jacob R. Marcus, *The Colonial American Jew, 1492–1776*, 3 vols. (Detroit, 1970), I, 215–48.
18. "Flushing Remonstrance," Dec. 27, 1657. E. B. O'Callaghan, ed., *Documents Relative to the Colonial History of the State of New York*, 15 vols. (Albany, 1856–83), XIV, 402–03. The language has been modernized.
19. *The New York Times*, Oct. 6, 1957.
20. April 16, 1663. Edwin T. Corwin, ed., *Ecclesiastical Records of the State of New York*, 7 vols. (Albany, 1901–16), I, 530.
21. *N. Y. Doc. Hist.*, I, 92; *Ecclesiastical Records*, II, 877–80.
22. John W. Pratt, *Religion, Politics, and Diversity: The Church-State Theme in New York History* (Ithaca, 1967), pp. 27–31.
23. David S. Lovejoy, "Equality and Empire: The New York Charter of Libertys, 1683," *William and Mary Quarterly*, 3rd ser., XXI (1964), 493–515, esp. 505–06.
24. Pratt, *Religion, Politics, and Diversity*, p. 38.
25. On the act, see R. T. Henshaw, "The New York Ministry Act of 1693," *Historical Magazine of the Protestant Episcopal Church*, II (1933), 199–204; and *Ecclesiastical Records*, II, 1076–79. The Rossiter quotation is from his "Shaping of the American Tradition," *William and Mary Quarterly*, 3rd ser., XI (1954), 522.

26. Rev. G. Du Bois to the Classis of Amsterdam, May 14, 1741, in *Ecclesiastical Records*, IV, 2756.
27. *The Journal of Madam [Sarah Kemble] Knight* (New York, 1920, 1935), p. 54; Carl Bridenbaugh, ed., *Gentleman's Progress: The Itinerarium of Dr. Alexander Hamilton* (Chapel Hill, 1948), p. 74. John Miller, an Anglican minister visiting New York in 1695, remarked of the inhabitants with unintended humor: "Their interests are their least concern, and, as if salvation were not a matter of moment, when they have opportunities of serving God they care not for making use thereof; or if they go to church, 'tis but too often out of curiosity, and to find faults in him that preacheth rather than to hear their own. . . ." A *Description of the Province and City of New-York* (London, 1695; new ed., John G. Shea, ed., 1862), pp. 38–39.
28. William Livingston and others, *The Independent Reflector*, Milton M. Klein, ed. (Cambridge, Mass., 1963), pp. 391, 396.
29. Perry Miller, "The Contribution of the Protestant Churches to Religious Liberty in Colonial America," *Church History*, IV (1935), 57–66; William G. McLoughlin, "Isaac Backus and the Separation of Church and State in America," *American Historical Review*, LXXIII (1968), 1392–1413; Pratt, *Religion, Politics, and Diversity*, Chapter 3.
30. Elkanah Watson, *Journal*, quoted in U. P. Hedrick, *A History of Agriculture in the State of New York* (New York, 1933, 1966), p. 65; *Independent Reflector*, pp. 94, 308.
31. Edgar J. McManus, *A History of Negro Slavery in New York* (Syracuse, 1966), Chapter 1.
32. *Ibid.*, pp. 126–36; John Hope Franklin, *From Slavery to Freedom*, 3rd ed. (New York, 1967), pp. 92–94; Winthrop D. Jordan, *White over Black: American Attitudes toward the Negro, 1550–1812* (Chapel Hill, 1968), pp. 115–18. The figures for those punished in the 1741 plot seem to vary in each modern account. Those above are taken from the list appended to Daniel Horsmanden's contemporary account, *A Journal of the Proceedings in the Detection of the Conspiracy. . .* (New-York, 1744), reprinted as *The New-York Conspiracy* (New York, 1810) and recently reprinted from the latter text with an introduction by Thomas J. Davis (Boston, 1971).
33. The quotations are from the 1971 edition of Horsmanden's *Journal*, pp. 105–06, 168. I cannot agree with Winthrop Jordan's conclusion that the social heterogeneity of the city and the politics of the colony created tensions that were palliated by vengeance against the Negroes (*White over Black*, pp. 119–20).
34. McManus, *Negro Slavery in New York*, Chapter 3.
35. Roi Ottley and William J. Weatherby, eds., *The Negro in New York: An Informal Social History* (New York, 1967), p. 34; Stanley A. Ransom, ed., *America's First Negro Poet . . . Jupiter Hammon of Long Island* (Port Washington, N. Y., 1970).
36. *The America of 1750: Peter Kalm's Travels in North America*, A. B. Benson, ed., 2 vols. (New York, 1937, 1964), I, 134; "Journal of Lord Adam Gordon," in Newton D. Mereness, ed., *Travels in the American Colonies* (New York, 1916), p. 414.

37. J. Hector St. John de Crevecoeur, *Letters from an American Farmer* (New York, 1957), pp. 37, 39.

38. Henry W. Dunshee, *History of the School of the Collegiate Dutch Church in the City of New York* (New York, 1883), p. 15; Joseph B. Bishop, *A Chronicle of One Hundred and Fifty Years: The Chamber of Commerce of the State of New York, 1768–1918* (New York, 1918), pp. 1–3; Lawrence H. Leder, "Robert Hunter's *Androborus*," *Bulletin* of the New York Public Library, LXVIII (March, 1964), 153-90; Richard H. Shryock, *Medicine and Society in America, 1600–1860* (New York, 1960; Ithaca, 1962), p. 33; Brooke Hindle, *The Pursuit of Science in Revolutionary America* (Chapel Hill, 1956), p. 110; A. R. Hasse, "The First Published Proceedings of an American Legislature," *The Bibliographer*, II (1903), 240–42.

39. Klein, "The Cultural Tyros of Colonial New York," *South Atlantic Quarterly*, LXVI (1967), 226; Hindle, *Science in Revolutionary America*, pp. 60–61; A. B. Keep, *The Library in Colonial New York* (New York, 1909), pp. 64–72; Shryock, *Medicine and Society*, pp. 22, 24–25; Paul M. Hamlin, *Legal Education in Colonial New York* (New York, 1939), pp. 96–97, 104 n.; L. H. Butterfield, ed., *Diary and Autobiography of John Adams*, 4 vols. (New York, 1964), I, 251–58.

40. Carl Bridenbaugh, *Cities in the Wilderness* (New York, 1964), pp. 289, 444, 449–50; Klein, "Church, State, and Education: Testing the Issue in Colonial New York," *New York History*, XLV (1964), 291–303. The reference in a New York indenture of November 25, 1690, to an evening school for the education of apprentices may make New York the originator of this unique American institution. See Robert F. Seybolt, *Apprenticeship and Apprenticeship Education in Colonial New York* (New York, 1917), p. 94, and *The Evening School in Colonial America* (Urbana, Ill., 1925), pp. 9–10, 15.

41. A. C. Flick, ed., *History of the State of New York*, 10 vols. (New York, 1933–37), III, 84–86; Hellmut Lehmann-Haupt and others, *The Book in America* (New York, 1939), pp. 31–32; Sidney Kobre, *The Development of the Colonial Newspaper* (Gloucester, Mass., 1960), pp. 147–48.

42. Thomas C. Cochran, "The Middle Atlantic Area in the Economic History of the United States," *Proceedings* of the American Philosophical Society, CVIII (April, 1964), 156–57; Roger W. Weiss, "The Issue of Paper Money in the American Colonies, 1720–1774," *Journal of Economic History*, XXX (1970), 770–84, esp. 777, 780; Gary M. Walton, "New Evidence on Colonial Commerce," *ibid.*, XXVIII (1968), 363–87.

43. H. L. Osgood, *The American Colonies in the Eighteenth Century*, 4 vols. (New York, 1924; Gloucester, Mass., 1958), I, x–xi.

44. Stanley Pargellis, "The Four Independent Companies of New York," in *Essays in Colonial History Presented to Charles McLean Andrews* (New Haven, 1931), pp. 96–123; Lawrence H. Leder, ed., "Dam'me Don't Stir a Man: Trial of New York Mutineers in 1700," *New York Historical Society Quarterly*, XLII (1958), 261–83; William A. Foote, "The American Independent Companies of the British Army, 1664–1764" (unpublished Ph.D. dissertation, UCLA, 1966), pp. 144–62, 245–82.

45. On the subject of New York in the strategy of empire, Max Savelle has

written most extensively and most recently and fully in his *Origins of
American Diplomacy* (New York, 1967), esp. 179–90 and 511–54. On
the post office, see William Smith, *History of the Post Office in British
North America, 1639–1870* (Cambridge, Engl., 1920), pp. 1, 19, 34.
46. J. H. Plumb, "Political Man," in James L. Clifford, ed., *Man Versus Society in Eighteenth-Century Britain* (Cambridge, Engl., 1968), p. 21.
47. Philip Padelford, ed., *Colonial Panorama: Dr. Robert Honeyman's Journal for March and April 1775* (San Marino, Calif., 1939), p. 31 (May
13, 1775).
48. Thomas Twining, quoted in Whitfield J. Bell, Jr., "The Middle States
Tradition in American Historiography: Introduction," *Proceedings* of
the American Philosophical Society, CVIII (April, 1964), 145; Theodore
Roosevelt, *New York* (New York, 1891, 1895), p. xi. Two articles which
treat the theme of New York's contribution to the development of the
nation are Allan Nevins, "The Golden Thread in the History of New
York," *New York Historical Society Quarterly,* XXXIX (1955), 5–22;
and Bayrd Still, "The Essence of New York City," *ibid.,* XLIII (1959),
401–23.

Patricia U. Bonomi (pages 29–50)

1. "The American Revolution: Revisions in Need of Revising," *William
and Mary Quarterly,* 3rd Ser., XIV (January, 1957), 3–15.
2. Kenneth A. Lockridge and Alan Kreider, "The Evolution of Massachusetts Town Government, 1640 to 1740," *WMQ,* 3rd Ser., XXIII (October 1966), 549–74; Kenneth Lockridge, *A New England Town: The
First Hundred Years* (New York, 1970); Sumner Chilton Powell, *Puritan Village: The Formation of a New England Town* (Middletown,
Conn., 1963); John J. Waters, "Hingham, Massachusetts, 1631–1661:
An East Anglian Oligarchy in the New World," *Journal of Social History,* I, No. 4, pp. 351–70; Philip J. Greven, Jr., *Four Generations:
Population, Land, and Family in Colonial Andover, Massachusetts* (Ithaca, 1970); John Demos, *A Little Commonwealth: Family Life in
Plymouth Colony* (New York, 1970).
3. Michael Zuckerman, *Peaceable Kingdoms: New England Towns in the
Eighteenth Century* (New York, 1970).
4. Charles S. Sydnor, *Gentlemen Freeholders: Political Practices in Washington's Virginia* (Chapel Hill, 1952); Robert E. and B. Katharine
Brown, *Virginia, 1705–1786: Democracy or Aristocracy?* (East Lansing,
Mich., 1964).
5. Gary B. Nash, *Quakers and Politics: Pennsylvania, 1681–1726* (Princeton, 1968); Sung Bok Kim, "A New Look at the Great Landlords of
Eighteenth-Century New York," *WMQ,* 3rd Ser., XXVII (October,
1970), 581–614; James T. Lemon, "Urbanization and the Development
of Eighteenth-Century Southeastern Pennsylvania and Adjacent Dela-
ware," *WMQ,* 3rd Ser., XXIV (October, 1967), 501–42; Milton M.
Klein, "Prelude to Revolution in New York: Jury Trials and Judicial
Tenure," *WMQ,* 3rd Ser., XVII (October, 1960), 439–62; Jerome I.

Nadelhaft, "Politics and the Judicial Tenure Fight in Colonial New Jersey," *WMQ*, 3rd Ser., XXVIII (January 1971), 46–63; James H. Hutson, "An Investigation of the Inarticulate: Philadelphia's White Oaks," *WMQ*, 3rd Ser., XXVII (January, 1971), 3–25; Stanley N. Katz, *Newcastle's New York: Anglo-American Politics, 1732–1753* (Cambridge, Mass., 1968).

6. Philip Livingston to Robert Livingston, Albany, Feb. 15, 1722, Livingston-Redmond MSS, Reel 3, FDR Library, Hyde Park.

7. This outline of local government is based on material from Patricia U. Bonomi, *A Factious People: Politics and Society in Colonial New York* (New York, 1971), pp. 28–39.

8. "A List of the Freeholders Within the County of Ulster, 1728," Edmund B. O'Callaghan, ed., *Documentary History of the State of New York* (Albany, 1849–51), III, 586.

9. Lockridge and Kreider, "Evolution of Massachusetts Town Government," p. 566.

10. *Perspectives in American History*, III (1969), 342.

11. Sidney and Beatrice Webb, *English Local Government from the Revolution to the Municipal Corporation Act: The Manor and Borough* (London, 1908), pp. 114–26, 200–11; *ibid.*, *The Parish and County*, 37n; F. W. Maitland, "The Survival of Archaic Communities," *Law Quarterly Review*, IX (July, 1893), 227, cited by Webbs, *op cit.*, *Parish and County*, 38n; W. E. Tate, *The Parish Chest: A Study of the Records of Parochial Administration in England* (Cambridge, 1946, 1969), p. 14.

12. This power to tax was abolished in 1834 when Parliament passed the Poor Law Amendment Act, the effect of which was to eliminate the parish as a viable unit of secular government. Webbs, *Parish and County*, pp. 171–72.

13. *Ibid.*, p. 5.

14. Tate, *Parish Chest*, p. 18; Webbs, *Parish and County*, p. 40.

15. Webbs, *Parish and County*, pp. 213–14.

16. *Ibid.*, p. 40; Tate, p. 18.

17. Powell, *Puritan Village*, pp. 13, 22.

18. *Ibid.*, p. 59.

19. Webbs, *Manor and Borough*, Chapters III, VI; Webbs, *Parish and County*, pp. 321–37.

20. Plumb, *England in the Eighteenth Century: 1714–1815* (Baltimore, 1950), pp. 36–37.

21. Thomas Middleton, *Blurt, Master Constable;* Henry Glapthorne, *Wit in a Constable;* Henry Fielding, *Amelia;* Tobias Smollett, *The Adventures of Sir Launcelot Greaves.*

22. "Records of the Town Court, Proceedings of the Trustees, etc. of Kingston, October 7, 1713–February 1737," Ulster County Records, New-York Historical Society.

23. "Records of . . . Trustees"; Marius Schoonmaker, *The History of Kingston, New York* (New York, 1888), pp. 139–42, 191. For Jan Post's farm, see "Records of . . . Trustees," Dec. 12, 1713.

24. "Records of . . . Trustees," May 7, 1718, Jan. 7, 1721, March 26, 1722,

April 26, 1723, March 2, 1728, April 9, 1729; Schoonmaker, *History of Kingston*, 140, 197–99.

25. Because most inhabitants of Kingston were of Dutch descent, the Dutch language may have been used more than English.
26. "Records of . . . Trustees," March 22, April 7, 1725.
27. The Board, or a part of it, also had a judicial function, as the trustees chose five of their number each year to sit monthly as a Town Court. This court handled problems having to do with strayed and impounded stock, money owed for land, and suits for debt. "Records of . . . Trustees," *passim*.
28. "Records of . . . Trustees," March 14, September 9, 1719.
29. "Records of . . . Trustees," March 2, 1714, March 4, 1717. Beside the Ten Broeck case, the only other evidence of reluctance to perform public duties is the 30s fine levied against chimney inspectors for refusal "to officiate said office." "Records of . . . Trustees," March 10, 1714.
30. "Records of . . . Trustees," June 27, 1726, March 29, 1727; Schoonmaker, *History of Kingston*, 194.
31. *Town of Bedford, Westchester County, New York: Historical Records* (Bedford, N.Y., 1966), I, "Minutes of Town Meetings, 1680–1737"; William G. Fulcher, comp., "Recorded Action Taken by Freeholders and Inhabitants of the Town of Mamaroneck as Found in the Town Record," Westchester County Historical Society *Quarterly Bulletin*, XIII (April, 1937), 39–48; Robert Bolton, *The History of the Several Towns, Manors, and Patents of the County of Westchester* (New York, 1881), II, 46–69.
32. "The Town and Mannor of Phillipsburgh Book, 1742–1773," *NYHS*.
33. "Phillipsburgh Town Book," 1773, *NYHS*.
34. See Bonomi, *A Factious People*, Chapter VI.
35. Even such appointive positions as Justices of the Peace were brought closer to the people in the eighteenth century when the governor's patronage was farmed out to various Assemblymen in the counties. Men appointed as Justices of the Peace, sheriffs, and county clerks in Westchester, Dutchess, and Albany counties were of the same stamp—solid and respectable, but often middle-class—as those appointed in such counties as Ulster.
36. Powell, *Puritan Village*, pp. 1–2.
37. Zuckerman, *Peaceable Kingdoms*, p. 229.
38. John R. Howe, Jr., "Republican Thought and the Political Violence of the 1790's," *American Quarterly*, XIX (Summer, 1967), 147–65.
39. Gordon S. Wood, *The Creation of the American Republic, 1776–1787* (Chapel Hill, N.C., 1969), p. 91.
40. Hannah Arendt, *On Revolution* (New York, 1963, 1965), pp. 144, 165.

Lawrence H. Leder (pages 51–56)

1. Lawrence H. Leder, "A Neglected Aspect of New York's Forgotten Century," *New York History*, XXXVII (1956), 259–65.

2. Frederick B. Tolles, "New Approaches to Research in Early American History," *William and Mary Quarterly*, 3d ser., XII (1955), 456–61.
3. Carl Bridenbaugh, "The Great Mutation," *American Historical Review*, LXVIII (1963), 322–23.

Thomas J. Archdeacon (pages 63–82)

1. Governor Dongan's Report on the State of the Province, 1687, in Edmund B. O'Callaghan, ed., *Documents Relative to the Colonial History of the State of New York* (Albany, 1853–57), III, 415. Hereafter cited as *Docs. Rel. Col. Hist. N.Y.*
2. Everts B. Greene and Virginia D. Harrington, *American Population before the Federal Census of 1790* (New York, 1932), p. 95. They estimated 813 males, 1,009 females, and 920 children.
3. These assessment records are available on microfilm at the Klapper Library of Queens College of the City University of New York.
4. Census of the City of New York [about the Year 1703], in Edmund B. O'Callaghan, ed., *Documentary History of the State of New York* (Albany, 1849), I, 611–24. Hereafter cited as *Doc. Hist. N.Y.*
5. Blacks in bondage, who unfortunately do not appear among the 876 heads of families, constituted the final segment of Manhattan's population; they comprised as much as 15 percent to 20 percent of the populace and were a silent minority exploited by their neighbors.
6. In order to simplify use of the assessment data, the various estimates of wealth expressed on the lists are grouped into five categories, each of which is large enough to hold approximately 20 percent of the population. Persons with the lowest valuations fall into the bottom category and those with the greatest wealth fit into the highest interval. Assigning a point value to each of the sections of the scale makes easy the description of the financial status of any individual in the population. Residents assessed on only £5 receive one point, on £10 or more two points, on £15 or more three, on £30 or more four, and on £70 or more five points.
7. Petition of the Mayor and Common Council of New York for a new Charter, Nov. 9, 1683, in O'Callaghan, ed., *Docs. Rel. Col. Hist. N.Y.*, III, 337–39.
8. Beverley McAnear, "The Place of the Freeman in Old New York," *New York History*, XXI (1940), 420. New York City, *Minutes of the Common Council* (New York, 1905), II, 163.
9. An Act for declareing Confirming & Explaining the Libertys of the City of New York relateing to ye Election of their Magistrats, May 1, 1702, New York Colony, *The Colonial Laws of New York, from the Year 1664 to the Revolution* (Albany, 1894), I, 490.
10. Stanley M. Pargellis, "Jacob Leisler," *Dictionary of American Biography*, VI, 156–57; Edwin R. Purple, *Genealogical Notes Relating to Lieut.-Gov. Jacob Leisler [and Loockermans]* (New York, 1877), pp. 7, 32.

11. Lawrence H. Leder, "Jacob Leisler and the New York Rebellion of 1689–1691" (unpublished Master's dissertation, New York University, 1950), p. 3; Edwin T. Corwin and H. Hastings, eds., *Ecclesiastical Records of the State of New York* (Albany, 1901), II, 800; James G. Wilson, *The Memorial History of the City of New York* (New York, 1893), I, 129.

12. Lieutenant Governor Leisler and Council to the Bishop of Salisbury, Jan. 7, 1690, in O'Callaghan, ed., *Docs. Rel. Col. Hist. N.Y.*, III, 654–55.

13. Captain Leisler to King William and Queen Mary, Aug. 20, 1689, in O'Callaghan, ed., *Docs. Rel. Col. Hist. N.Y.*, III, 615.

14. Purple, *Genealogical Notes . . . Leisler*, pp. 7, 12; Herbert L. Osgood, *The American Colonies in the Eighteenth Century* (New York, 1924), III, 459; [Mrs.] Schuyler Van Rensselaer, *History of the City of New York in the Seventeenth Century* (New York, 1909), II, 241; Hamilton Fish, *Anthon Genealogy* (New York, 1930), pp. 55–56.

15. Fish, *Anthon Genealogy*, pp. 55–56; Rev. W. E. De Riemer, *The De Riemer Family* (New York, 1905), pp. 7–8; Jonathan Pearson, "Staats Genealogy," *New York Genealogical and Biographical Record*, II (1871), 140–41.

16. Colonel Bayard's Narrative of Occurrences in New York, from April to December, 1689, December 13, 1689; A Memoriall of What Has Occurred in Their Maties Province of New York since the News of Their Majties Arrivall in England, n.d., both in O'Callaghan, ed., *Docs. Rel. Col. Hist. N.Y.*, III, 639, II, 58.

17. Appointment of Leisler's Council, Dec. 11, 1689, in O'Callaghan, ed., *Doc. Hist. N.Y.*, II, 45.

18. George F. Rudé, *The Crowd in History: A Study of Popular Disturbances in France and England, 1730–1848* (New York, 1964), Chapter IX.

19. The Narrative [of Nicholas Bayard], Jan. 21, 1690, in O'Callaghan, ed., *Docs. Rel. Col. Hist. N.Y.*, III, 681–82.

20. Petition of Gabriel Minvielle to Governor Sloughter, n.d., in O'Callaghan, ed., *Doc. Hist. N.Y.*, II, 371; Edwin R. Purple, "Varleth Family," *Contributions to the History of Ancient Families of New Amsterdam and New York* (New York, 1881), p. 89.

21. The Narrative [of Nicholas Bayard], Jan. 21, 1690, in O'Callaghan, ed., *Docs. Rel. Col. Hist. N.Y.*, III, 673; New York County, Conveyance Libers, XIII, 225–26 (notes Vanderburgh's occupation); Corporation of Trinity Church, Minutes of the Vestry, I (1697–1791), 46.

22. Governor Sloughter to Lord Nottingham, May 6, 1691, in O'Callaghan, ed., *Docs. Rel. Col. Hist. N.Y.*, III, 760.

23. Earl of Bellomont to the Lords of Trade, April 27, 1699; Earl of Bellomont to the Lords of the Treasury, May 25, 1698; Earl of Bellomont to the Lords of Trade, June 22, 1698, all in O'Callaghan, ed., *Docs. Rel. Col. Hist. N.Y.*, IV, 508, 317, 325–26.

24. Earl of Bellomont to the Lords of the Treasury, May 25, 1698; Heads of Accusation against the Earl of Bellomont, March 11, 1700, in

O'Callaghan, ed., *Docs. Rel. Col. Hist. N.Y.*, IV, 317–18, 620–23; John D. Runcie, "The Problem of Anglo-American Politics in Bellomont's New York," *William and Mary Quarterly*, 3d Ser., XXVI, #2 (April 1969), 205–06, 210; Col. Nicholas Bayard to Sir Philip Meadows, March 8, 1701, in O'Callaghan, ed., *Docs. Rel. Col. Hist. N.Y.*, IV, 848.
25. New York City, *Minutes of the Common Council of the City of New York, 1675–1776* (New York, 1905), II, 159–76.
26. *Ibid.*, pp. 163–76.

Edwin G. Burrows (pages 83–92)

1. Orin G. Libby, *The Geographical Distribution of the Vote of the Thirteen States on the Federal Constitution, 1787–8* (Madison, Wisc., 1894); Charles A. Beard, *An Economic Interpretation of the Constitution of the United States* (New York, 1913). Among recent studies, see especially Forrest McDonald, *We the People: The Economic Origins of the Constitution* (Chicago, 1958); Lee Benson, *Turner and Beard: American Historical Writing Reconsidered* (Glencoe, Ill., 1960); Jackson Turner Main, *The Antifederalists: Critics of the Constitution* (Chapel Hill, N. C., 1961); and Main, "Charles A. Beard and the Constitution: A Critical Review of Forrest McDonald's *We the People*," with a rebuttal by McDonald, *William and Mary Quarterly*, 3d. ser., 17 (1960), 86–110. William O. Aydelotte, *Quantification in History* (Reading, Mass., 1971), is a useful general introduction to methodological issues.
2. There are, of course many notable examples of constructive quantification, particularly of late in the field of historical demography. My point is only that, for one reason or another, such examples can no longer be found among studies in one of the first areas where quantification appeared.
3. The collective-biographical, or prosopographical, analysis of ratifying conventions is perhaps the most common way quantification-minded historians have tried to find correlations between what Federalists and Antifederalists thought and the kinds of people they were. It is not the only strategy available, nor the best for all purposes, but it does avoid the often awkward business of sample-taking and suits a political culture in which the opinion of elites weighed more heavily than that of the electorate. The former point needs emphasis: the candidates under study here are not a sample of anything and cannot be treated as such. For a general discussion, see Lawrence Stone, "Prosopography," *Daedalus* (Winter, 1972), 46–79.
4. The sources for these data include the New York State Historian's *Second Annual Report, 1896* (Albany, 1897), and *Third Annual Report, 1897* (Albany, 1898), both containing colonial muster rolls; "Muster Rolls of New York Provincial Troops, 1755–1764," *Collections of the New-York Historical Society for the Year 1891* (New York, 1892); "Revolutionary Muster Rolls, Volume II (1775–83)," *Collections of the New-York Historical Society for the Year 1915* (New York, 1916),

338–511; and the rolls in Berthold Fernow, *New York in the Revolution*
(Albany, 1887), and in James A. Roberts, *New York in the Revolution*
(Albany, 1898). Also Francis B. Heitman, *Historical Register of Officers
of the Continental Army* (Washington, 1914). The colonial rolls reveal
that only a handful of men on either side of the ratification question
had held militia commissions prior to 1774.

5. Even in those areas reporting Antifederalist majorities in the election,
for example, Federalist candidates were still far more likely to have
served in the Continentals than in the militia. The need to test for spu-
rious correlations of this sort underscores the value of including unsuc-
cessful as well as successful candidates for the convention in the study
—a consideration usually overlooked in collective-biographical analyses
of ratifying conventions.

6. Robert K. Merton, "Patterns of Influence: Local and Cosmopolitan Influentials," *Social Theory and Social Structure* (Glencoe, Ill., 1957), pp.
387–420. The utility of this splendid essay for historians has been discussed by Samuel P. Hays, "Political Parties and the Community-Soci-
ety Continuum," in William Nisbet Chambers and Walter Dean Burn-
ham, eds., *The American Party Systems: Stages of Political Development* (New York, 1967), pp. 152–81.

7. New York's principal militia statutes before 1789 are reproduced in fac-
simile in Arthur Vollmer, *Military Obligation: The American Tradition*
[Selective Service System, Special Monograph Series 1, v. II], Part 9
(Washington, 1947). See especially the acts of 1772, 1775, 1778, and
1782. For general background, consult Peter Nelson, "Military Organi-
zations and Activities," in Alexander Flick, ed., *History of the State of
New York*, 10 vols. (New York, 1933), IV, 3–31, and Roberts, *New
York in the Revolution*, pp. 1–15.

8. [New York State Division of Archives and History], *The Revolution in
New York* (Albany, 1926), p. 159; Alexander Flick, "The Sullivan-Clin-
ton Campaign of 1779," in Flick, ed., *History of New York*, IV, 213.
The names of future Antifederalists appear often in local accounts of
British depradations, and it would seem that the "atrocity story" formed
still another part of their common experiences.

9. See, e.g., the remarks in the Poughkeepsie convention by Gilbert Livingston and Thomas Tredwell: Jonathan Elliot, comp., *Debates in the Several State Conventions on the Adoption of the Federal Constitution*, 5
vols. (Philadelphia, 1836), II, 286, 403–04.

10. See, e.g., "Cato" [George Clinton?], as reprinted in Paul Leicester
Ford, ed., *Essays on the Constitution of the United States* (New York,
1892), p. 259. Cecilia Kenyon has discussed this thinking as a general
ideological formulation in the invaluable introduction to her collection,
The Antifederalists (Indianapolis, 1966), pp. xxxix–xlviii. Cf. William A.
Benton, "Pennsylvania Revolutionary Officers and the Federal Constitution," *Pennsylvania History*, 31 (1964), 419–35.

11. See, e.g., remarks by John Lansing and Melancton Smith in Elliot, *Debates*, II, 245–21, 261–62, 373–74.

12. On imitation and orthodoxy, consult Russel F. Weigley, *Towards an*

Notes   [*143*]

American Army: Military Thought from Washington to Marshall (New
York, 1962), pp. 1–29; and the same author's *History of the United
States Army* (New York, 1967), pp. 29–94.
13. This aspect of the Army's function is a largely unexplored topic. Sey-
mour Martin Lipset has shown the importance of the commander-in-
chief's national charisma, but only for the years after 1789: *The First
New Nation* (New York, 1963), esp., pp. 15ff. I profited from the essays in John J. Johnston, ed., *The Role of the Military in Underdeveloped Countries* (Princeton, 1962); and from S. N. Eisenstadt's concept
of the "solidarity symbol" presented in his "Political Development," in
Amitai and Eva Etzioni, eds., *Social Change* (New York, 1964), pp.
310–23. On "rationalizing" the use of national resources, see F. X. Sut-
ton, "Analyzing Social Systems," and Neil J. Smelser, "Mechanisms of
Change and Adjustment to Change," in Jason L. Finkle and Richard W.
Gable, eds., *Political Development and Social Change* (New York,
1966), pp. 19–28, 28–43. Cf. remarks by Hamilton and Jay in Elliot,
Debates, II, 347ff. and 380ff.
14. See, e.g., comments by Jay and Madison in *The Federalist*, Modern Library ed. (New York, n.d.), pp. 9, 84.
15. Morris, "The Confederation Period and the American Historian," *William and Mary Quarterly*, 3d. ser., XIII (1956), 139. Philip Schuyler to
Peter Van Schaack, March 13, 1787: Henry C. Van Schaack, ed., *Life
of Peter Van Schaack* (New York, 1842), pp. 149–55; Washington to
Jay, May 13, 1786: H. P. Johnston, ed., *Correspondence and Public
Papers of Jay*, 4 vols. (New York, 1891), III, 195–96.
16. See, e.g., Louis Gottschalk, ed., *The Letters of Lafayette to Washington*
(New York, 1944), *passim*.
17. *The Federalist*, pp. 156–57. For other discussions of military subjects,
see Numbers 4, 8, 11, 22–29, 41, and 46.
18. *Ibid.*, pp. 14–15, 49, 60, 167, 330, 349–53, 359–65, 365–70; 370–76;
Elliot, *Debates*, II, 265–67, 275, 283, 302–03, 345.
19. Nor that such a division existed in the electorate at large. The body of
convention candidates, once again, should not be mistaken as a sample
of some larger collectivity.

FURTHER READINGS

Carl L. Becker, *The History of Political Parties in the Province of New York, 1760–1776* (Madison, Wisc., 1909).

Patricia U. Bonomi, *A Factious People; Politics and Society in Colonial New York* (New York, 1971).

George Dangerfield, *Chancellor Robert R. Livingston of New York 1746–1813* (New York, 1960).

Linda Grant DePauw, *The Eleventh Pillar: New York State and the Federal Constitution* (Ithaca, N. Y., 1966).

David M. Ellis, et al., *History of New York State* (Ithaca, N. Y., 1967).

Stanley N. Katz, *Newcastle's New York; Anglo-American Politics, 1732–1753* (Cambridge, Mass., 1968).

Lawrence H. Leder, *Robert Livingston, 1654–1728, and the Politics of Colonial New York* (Chapel Hill, N. C., 1961).

Staughton Lynd, *Class Conflict, Slavery and the United States Constitution* (New York, 1968).

Edgar J. McManus, *A History of Negro Slavery in New York* (Syracuse, N. Y., 1966).

Bernard Mason, *The Road to Independence* (Lexington, Ky., 1966).

E. Wilder Spaulding, *New York in the Critical Period, 1783–1789* (New York, 1932).

Sung Bok Kim, "A New Look at the Great Landlords of Eighteenth Century New York," *William and Mary Quarterly*, 3d Ser., XXVII (October, 1970), 581–614.

Philip L. White, *The Beekmans of New York in Politics and Commerce, 1647–1877* (New York, 1956).

Alfred F. Young, *The Democratic Republicans of New York* (Chapel Hill, N. C., 1967).

CONTRIBUTORS

THOMAS J. ARCHDEACON, formerly a member of the faculty at the United States Military Academy at West Point, is currently on the faculty of the University of Wisconsin at Madison.

PATRICIA U. BONOMI is Associate Professor of History at New York University. She is the author of *A Factious People: Politics and Society in Colonial New York*.

EDWIN G. BURROWS is a member of the History Department of Brooklyn College of the City University of New York. He previously taught at Herbert H. Lehman College and at Marymount College, Tarrytown, New York. He is the author, with Michael Wallace, of "The American Revolution: The Ideology and Psychology of National Liberation," *Perspectives in American History*, VI (1972).

MILTON M. KLEIN is Professor of History at the University of Tennessee. He has been a Ford Foundation Traveling Fellow, a Fulbright lecturer, and a Clements Library Fellow. Professor Klein edited *The Independent Reflector*, is the author of "The Rise of the New York Bar: The Legal Career of William Livingston," and contributed to *The Colonial Legacy* edited by Lawrence H. Leder. He is currently preparing an annotated bibliography on New York in the American Revolution.

LAWRENCE H. LEDER, Chairman of the Department of History of Lehigh University, formerly taught at Brandeis University and Louisiana State University in New Orleans. He also served as Research Associate at Sleepy Hollow Restorations. Professor Leder was the recipient of an award of merit from the American Association for State and Local History and of the Annual Manuscript Award of the Institute of Early American History and Culture for his study, *Robert Livingston and the Politics of Colonial New York*. In addition to numerous articles on early New York affairs, he is the author of *The Livingston Indian Records; Liberty and Authority*, and *America 1603–1789: Prelude to a Nation*. He currently is a member of the Board of Directors of Historic Bethlehem Incorporated.

Jackson T. Main, Professor of History and Director of the Institute for Colonial Studies at the State University of New York at Stony Brook, formerly taught at Washington and Jefferson College, University of Maryland, and San Jose State College. A former member of the Council of the Institute of Early American History and Culture, he is the author of *The Antifederalists; The Social Structure of Revolutionary America; The Upper House in Revolutionary America;* and, *The Antifederalists: Critics of the Constitution*. His most recent work is *Political Parties Before the Constitution*.

Richard B. Morris is Gouverneur Morris Professor of History at Columbia University. He has been a Fulbright Scholar and a Columbia University Guggenheim Fellow. Professor Morris has served as the Chairman of the New York City Task Force in Municipal Archives, and as a member of the American Revolution Bicentennial Commission. Among his many publications are *Government and Labor in Early America; The Peacemakers,* recipient of the Bancroft Prize; *John Jay, The Nation and The Court; Alexander Hamilton & The Founding of the Nation; The American Revolution Reconsidered;* and, *Emerging Nations & The American Revolution,* and *Seven Who Shaped Our Destiny*.

Editors

Jacob Judd is a member of the faculty of Herbert H. Lehman College of the City University of New York and is the Research Coordinator for Sleepy Hollow Restorations. He has contributed numerous articles pertaining to New York history to the *New York Historical Society Quarterly, New York History* and *The Journal of Long Island History*. Professor Judd is the author of *Fort Lee on the Palisades*.

Irwin H. Polishook, author of *Rhode Island & The Union, 1774–1795;* and *Roger Williams, John Cotton & Religious Freedom: A Controversy in New & Old England,* is a member of the faculty of Herbert H. Lehman College. He has been a Brown University Fellow, a Hearst Fellow at Northwestern University, and a recipient of a Social Science Research Council fellowship.

INDEX

A

Adams, Charles Francis, 51
Adams, Henry, 28
Adams, James Truslow, 51
Adams, John, 103, 117
Adams, Samuel, 103
Agriculture, in New York, 5,
  25–26
Albany, 33
Albany County, 46
Albany Plan of 1754, 104
Alexander, James, 26, 52
Alsop, John, 102
André, Major John, 114
Andrews, Charles M., 51
Andros, Edmond, Governor, 19,
  71
Anglican Church, in New York, 20
Antifederalists, 60–61, 83–92
Anti-Leislerians, 70–82
Archdeacon, Thomas J., vii, 58,
  60, 63–82, 93
Arendt, Hannah, 48–49
Articles of Capitulation, 19
Articles of Confederation, 61
Assessment rolls, Manhattan,
  66–67

B

Backus, Isaac, 21
Bailyn, Bernard, 51
Battle of New York, 113
Bayard, Nicholas, 73
Beard, Charles A., 60, 83
Becker, Carl, 15, 96
Bedford, 45
Bellomont, Earl of, 75
Benton, William A., 93
Bonomi, Patricia U., vii, 6–7,
  29–50, 51, 54
Boorstin, Daniel, 16
Borough, in England, 39–40
Boston, 24, 93
Bridenbaugh, Carl, 55

Bruce, Philip A., 51
Burnet, William, 52
Burrows, Edwin G., vii, 58,
  60–61, 83–92, 93

C

Carmichael, William, 99–100
Census, 1703, Manhattan, 64
Chartered city, in New York, 33
Clarke, George, 52
Colden, Cadwallader, 24, 26, 52
Collective biography, 60–61
Colve, Anthony, Governor, 71
Commerce, in New York, 23
Computer, and historical
  materials, 57–62
Constitution of 1787, 61
Continental Army, 61, 84–92
Continental Congress, 103,
  106–107, 110
Cooper, James Fenimore, 115
Cortlandt Manor, 45
Cosmopolitan-localist dichotomy,
  84–87, 92–93
County Government, in New
  York Colony, 32
Craven, Wesley, 8, 52
Crevecoeur, 23
Culture, in New York, 24

D

Dabney, Virginius, 8
Deane, Silas, 103, 109
Declaration of Independence,
  111–112
De La Noy, Pieter, 72
Demos, John, 51, 58
DePeyster, Abraham, 52
Dickinson, John, 103–104,
  106–107, 109
Donald, David, 13
Dongan, Thomas, Governor, 63
Duane, James, 110, 115

147

Dutch settlers, in Manhattan,
  66–67
Dutchess County, 32, 44, 46

E

Economic stratification, in New
  York, 1703, 67
Education, in New York, 23, 25
Elections, Manhattan, 1700's,
  69–70, 77–81
Edsall, Samuel, 72
England, 6, 10, 16, 20, 26, 27,
  37–41, 47, 104–105
English settlers, in Manhattan,
  66–67
Ethnic composition, New York,
  1700's, 66
Evans, Lewis, 12

F

The Federalist, 91
Federalists, 60–61, 83–92
Fiske, John, 11–12
Fletcher, Benjamin, Governor, 75
Flexner, James T., 54
Flippen, Percy, 52
Flushing remonstrance, 17–19
Fort Amsterdam, 1
Fort Orange, 1
Franklin, Benjamin, 104, 107
French and Indian Wars, 26
French settlers, in Manhattan,
  66–67

G

Galloway, Joseph, 104
Geography, as reason for neglect-
  ing study of Middle Atlantic
  region, 12
George III, 108
Georgia, 16
Gordon, William, 11
Greene, Evarts Boutwell, 64
Greven, Philip, 51, 58

H

Hamilton, Alexander, 91
Hammon, Jupiter, 22–23
Hansen, Marcus Lee, 12

Harrington, Virginia, 64
Harris, P. M. G., 37
Haskins, George L., 51
Henretta, James A., 93
Henry, Patrick, 11, 103–104
Hindle, Brooke, vii
Hobsbawm, Eric, 74
Howe, John, 48
Howe, Lord Richard, 112
Howe, Sir William, 112
Hudson River, 5
Hunter, Robert, Governor, 24, 52
Huguenots, 21, 66

I

Immigration, studies of, 12
Indians, lack of conflict with, in
  New York, 13
Irving, Washington, 11

J

Jay, James, 98, 109
Jay, John, 96–117
Jay, Sally, 100–101
Jefferson, Thomas, 21, 99
Jews, in New York, 12, 17, 64
Johnson, E. A. J., 51
Johnson, Sir William, 52, 54
Jones, Thomas, 11
Judd, Jacob, viii, 1–7, 54
Justices of the Peace, 37

K

Kalm, Peter, 23
Katz, Stanley, 54
Kennedy, Alexander, 26
Kingston, N. Y., town government
  of, 6–7, 34–44; Board of
  Trustees, 1711–1776, 118–131
Kittredge, E. L., 51
Klein, Milton M., vii, 5–6, 8–28,
  51, 52, 54, 55

L

Laight, Edward, 101
Laight, William, 104–105
Leder, Lawrence H., vii, 6, 51–56,
  62
Lee, Richard Henry, 104, 111

Legislative records, 58
Leisler, Jacob, 60, 70–82
Libby, Orin G., 83
Libraries, in New York, 24
Livingston, Gilbert, 113
Livingston, Henry Brockholst, 98–99
Livingston Manor, 33, 113
Livingston, Philip, 33
Livingston, Robert, 62, 100, 115
Livingston, William, 11, 26, 52, 100, 104
Local government in New York, 6; compared with Old England, 37–41
Lockridge, Kenneth, 51, 58
Long Island, 32, 113

M

McDonald, Forrest, 93
McDougall, Alexander, 102, 108, 110, 115
Madison, James, 91
Main, Jackson Turner, vii, 58, 93–95
Mamaroneck, 45
Manors, in New York colony, 33, 44–45
Manumission Society, New York, 116
Massachusetts, 10, 16, 25, 63, 71
Mereness, Newton, 52
Merton, Robert K., 61, 84, 86, 92
Middle Colonies, 8, 12–16; urban character of, 13–14; paucity of studies of, 51, 54
Milborne, Jacob, 72–73
Military service, effect on attitude toward ratification, 84–92
Miller, Perry, 51
Minvielle, Gabriel, 74
Morgan, Edmund, 29, 36, 51
Morison, Samuel Eliot, 51
Morris, Gouverneur, 111, 115
Morris, Richard B., vii, 90, 96–117
Morrisania Manor, 45–46
Mulford, Samuel, 52
Murdock, Kenneth, 51

N

Namier, Sir Lewis B., 61
Negroes, in New York, 22–23, 42, 116
New Amsterdam, 1
New England, 10–13, 30, 51, 71
New Jersey, 11, 12
New Netherland, 2, 16
New York, as colony, neglect of by historians, 8–11, 63
New York, municipality, 1–7, 33, 63–70
New York, province, 1–7, 63
New York State Ratifying Convention, 1787, 61, 84
Nicolls, Richard, 1, 19

O

O'Callaghan, Edmund B., 64
Occupations, in New York, 1700's, 69
Orange County, 32, 74
Osgood, Herbert L., 26

P

Paine, Thomas, 117
Parish, in England, 38–39
Parochialism, in local politics, 49-50
Patents, in New York Colony, 44–45
Pennsylvania, 11, 12
Philadelphia, 13, 23, 24, 93
Philipse, Adolph, 2, 5
Philipse, Frederick, 2, 5, 46
Philipsburgh Manor, 45–46
Plumb, J. H., 28, 40
Polishook, Irwin H., viii, 57–62
Politics, in New York, 4, 27–28
Population, heterogeneity in New York, 16, 64–66
Powell, Sumner Chilton, 39, 40, 47, 51
Precincts, 33
Press, in New York, 25
Prosopography, or collective biography, 61

Q
Quakers, in New York, 17–19
Quantification, and New York
   history, 57–62

R
Racial violence, in New York,
   21–22
Rebellion, Leisler's, 73–82
Religious tolerance, in New York,
   16–22
Republicanism, in local politics,
   47–50
Residential patterns, in
   Manhattan, 1703, 67
Revolutionary War, 87, 112–117
Roosevelt, Theodore, 28
Rossiter, Clinton, 20
Rudé, George, 74
Rutledge, Edward, 104, 112
Rutledge, John, 106
Rye, 45

S
Schlesinger, Arthur, Jr., 57–58
Schuyler, Peter, 52
Scott, John Morin, 11, 102
Shryock, Richard, 12
Slavery, in New York, 22–23, 42,
   116
Sloughter, Henry, Governor, 75
Smith, William, 52, 54
South, 11, 51
The Spy, 115
State militia, New York, 61,
   84–92
Steiner, B. C., 52
Stuyvesant, Peter, 4, 17–19
Suffolk Resolves, 103
Sydnor, Charles, 30, 37

T
Tate, W. E., 39

Thomson, Charles, 103
Tocqueville, Alexis de, 49
Tolles, Frederick, 52
Tories, 104–105
Townships, in New York Colony,
   32–33
Turner, Frederick Jackson,
   14–15, 26

U
Ulster County, 32, 33–34
Upton, L. F. S., 54
Urban character, Middle
   Colonies, 13–14

V
Virginia, 10, 13, 63
Voting, in Manhattan, 1701,
   69–70

W
Washington, George, 11
Waters, John, 51
Webb, Sidney and Beatrice,
   38–39
Wertenbaker, Thomas J., 12,
   51–52
West India Company, 1
Westchester County, 5, 32, 44,
   54, 74, 113
Whigs, 101, 104–105
Williamsburg, 10
Wilson, Woodrow, 15
Winthrop, Robert C., 51
Wood, Gordon, 48
Woodward, C. Vann, 13
Wright, Louis B., 52
Wythe, George, 109

Y
York, Duke of, 1, 19

Z
Zuckerman, Michael, 30, 47

Sleepy Hollow Restorations, Inc., is a nonprofit educational institution chartered by the State of New York. Established under an endowment provided by the late John D. Rockefeller, Jr., Sleepy Hollow Restorations owns and maintains Van Cortlandt Manor, in Croton-on-Hudson, a distinguished eighteenth-century family residence, and Sunnyside, Washington Irving's picturesque home in Tarrytown. Most recently, Sleepy Hollow Restorations completed the reconstruction of Philipsburg Manor, Upper Mills, at its original site on the Pocantico River, an impressive example of a colonial commercial-mill complex.